THE CREATION OF WEALTH

Using
Enterprise and Increasing Returns
to Scale

BY
TIM WALSHAW

ISBN: 978-0-6459786-7-4

CONTENTS

FIGURES

TABLES

INTRODUCTION

You need <u>both</u> *Enterprise* and *Increasing Returns to Scale* to create wealth. "Enterprise" is setting up the firm. "Increasing Returns to Scale" is a process of operating the firm. Enterprise alone won't make it, as you also need something to sell, produced at a steadily falling cost. In other words, your firm needs to become large enough to operate under "increasing returns to scale" to make substantial profits. If your firm is too small, you don't create new wealth. Also, once you achieve increasing returns to scale, sales prices and marketing are a secondary consideration.

Many thousands of books have been written about how to get rich. They say basically the same thing. Save, and then invest wisely. In property, shares, etc. Some authors add additional precepts. "Use other peoples' money".

It all sounds very clever. Yes, if a person saves and invests wisely, and if they borrow wisely, they can become moderately well off. But investing in shares means that you only get a small fraction of the profits. The rest gets swept elsewhere to the managers and the inside crowd. Unless you run a successful investment fund. And then again, that is running your own business.

This book is about *creating* new wealth, not *obtaining* wealth. Yes, Atilla the Hun obtained great wealth. You can obtain wealth by robbery, extortion, theft, violence, piracy, speculation, gambling. But experience shows that the chance of successfully achieving this, despite fictional accounts, is small.

So how do the rich become rich, and the poor remain poor? I mean rich as Rockefeller, or Bill Gates? Exploitation? Hard work? Luck? Being in the right place at the right time?

Is there some secret that allows you, without capital, excessive effort, or luck, become very rich?

Yes, there is. And this secret is described by the dual concepts – "Enterprise", combined with "Increasing Returns to Scale". If you combine Enterprise, which is starting and owning a firm, that firm must produce goods or services for sale under Increasing Returns to Scale. And together with the necessary hard work, leadership, and good management - yes, the usual stuff, you will become, depending on the size of the market, rich. If it is a large market, you could become very rich. If it is a global market with a major demand for your product, very, very, rich.

However, to repeat, you have to *both* start a new enterprise and operate the firm under increasing returns to scale. If you are just enterprising, and maybe start a small firm, and/or the firm does not operate under increasing returns to scale, you will <u>not</u> become rich, regardless of hard work, leadership and good management. You need <u>both</u> enterprise and increasing returns to scale together at the same time.

If, despite all those self-help books, you just offer hard work, leadership and good management alone, you will not become rich. While those are exemplary qualities, they are not by themselves the road to wealth. If you work for someone else or you own a small business, you will only make a reasonable living, at best. Both enterprise and increasing returns to scale are defined in detail later in this book.

Real estate? You invest in real estate <u>after</u> you have got rich. Investing in real estate only works when both population and income is expanding in that locality. Also, there can be technological changes even in real estate, such as reduced demand for office space in city centres. Real estate values can and do fall. Real estate is not an automatic road to wealth. Furthermore, leveraged investment can be highly risky.

I must warn that not everyone everywhere inhabits the economic and political environment to become rich the way I recommend. To create wealth, you must live or operate in a nation with a free and open market, a respect for private property, and an efficient and honest legal system. Since most parts of the globe do not have these requirements, you must go to one of the nations that display these properties if you wish to fully benefit from your entrepreneurial activities.

What you don't need to get rich are things that are often quoted – low labour costs, plentiful resources, low interest rates, a lot of funds to borrow, a low cost location (though that certainly helps)……. In the right political and economic environment (see above) you can get rich with high labor costs, limited resources, limited funds to borrow, and a high cost location. But you <u>do</u> need a reasonably large market. But if the business environment is bad, you can always move your firm to a better location when you can afford it. For example, the original industrial revolution started in the eighteenth century in north England, in an out of the way valley, the only asset being a fast running river to power a cotton mill. Cotton cloth production was moved to the town of Manchester, in the north-west of England when steam engines became viable, as this city had access to coal and better transport facilities.

What I am going to talk about in this book is the method where **everybody** wins. You, the workers, society, everybody is better off. There are no losers. Wealth is increased for you individually, and in total, everybody else in the world.

So how is wealth created? Yes, from nothing. No capital needed. We will discuss it all, starting with the next Chapter.

PART I

ECONOMIC THEORY AND THE THEORY OF INCREASING RETURNS

In Part I, we concentrate on basic economic theory. Why? Because if you do not understand how the world and your firm will work, you will make many mistakes. Some of these mistakes will be large, and terminal. Some will be small, and maybe you will learn from them. But saying "I live in an economic world. I know how economics works" is foolish and wrong. At this point, can you tell the difference between increasing returns to scale and decreasing returns to scale? This is vital information, believe me, that you will need to keep in mind at all times. What is the best sales strategy for long term survival? Supply and demand? No. It is selling as much as you can at a lower than market price but at a long-term constant price. Believe me.

If your firm is to survive and prosper, you must be thoroughly aware of the economic axioms described in these pages, and practice them always. Or don't bother going into business. You are heading for failure.

Bear with me. Towards the end of Part I you will say "Oh, I didn't know that! Now I know!" So, onward to the explanation of increasing returns to scale.

CHAPTER ONE

SUPPLY

We need to start with basic economic theory. Otherwise, the reader will soon come to the point of saying "Why?". You need an understanding of the basic process of making wealth. As most readers will have a limited comprehension of economic theory, we need to start at the beginning, but we will describe only the relevant part. We will start with the theory of Supply, not Demand. How to set up a firm, even if there is minimal demand. Then make it grow.

Most textbooks start with the theory of Demand. In the opinion of the author, the theory of Demand is far less important than the theory of Supply. Supply must come first. "Assuming" goods and services exist first, to be demanded and paid for is nonsense. The economy needs to be theoretically built up from the start. Like the chicken and the egg, supply exists before demand.

All businesses supply things that are hopefully sold at a profit. If the business does not make a profit, your business ceases to exist.

Now, is going into business an automatic source of wealth? No. Is the owner of a small shop wealthy? No, not really. Is the owner of a single truck wealthy? No, not really. Even owning and operating a farm, in most cases, is not a source of wealth. All these small businesses are called by economists "Buying yourself a job". You don't get rich, no matter how hard you work.

So, what is the difference between a small shop and a department store. Yes, more sales. But how do you get more sales? Employ more people. Many more people. And yes, operate efficiently, and divide the operations into many different specialist parts, and get the employees to specialise. It is what Adam Smith in his book "The Wealth of Nations" (1776) defined as the "Division of Labor".

This is what economists call "Increasing Returns to Scale".

Thus, the owner of a department store is rich, a lot richer than the owner of a single store, even though they are in the same business. The department store has many different departments specialising in different good for sale, and these departments employ sales people who specialise selling different types of goods. The outcome is the same regardless of what sort of business you are in. Some areas of the firm specialise in production, others in sales and so on. Oil, software, manufacturing…..Get big, but only in a certain way, different areas specialise in different activities.

A bit more economics. A small one-man business operates under "Constant Returns to Scale". If he hires an employee, he could continue operating under constant returns to scale, or he could get lucky and operate under the aforementioned increasing returns to scale, or he could be unlucky enough to operate under "Decreasing Returns to Scale" due to bad management. This will limit his possible growth, or even send his business broke.

Is there a deeper explanation?

Now we dive into economics, from its basic description of supply.

Supply is the supply of goods or services for sale. To start with basic theory, it is initially assumed that it is sold at a fixed price per unit. (However later on in economic theory, the price could vary. Another assumption is that when the price falls more goods and services are sold, and when the price rises less goods are sold. Good old "supply and demand").

Let's start with a small business. It operates at constant returns to scale. We now go to one of the basic tools of economics, the two axis-geometric figure.

Before we go onto prices and costs, the first two axis diagram we use is where the 'y' axis is quantity output and the 'x' axis is quantity input, for a particular firm. Both output and input are aggregates of constant proportions of individual goods.

Under Constant Returns to Scale, for each unit quantity of input, there is a unit quantity of output. Now what is important is the rate of increase. Under the 'technical' characteristics of Constant Returns to Scale, output increases at the same rate as Input. As can be seen in the diagram below, if the level of input is related to the level of output, it traces a straight line which is at 45°.

Figure one   Constant Returns to Scale

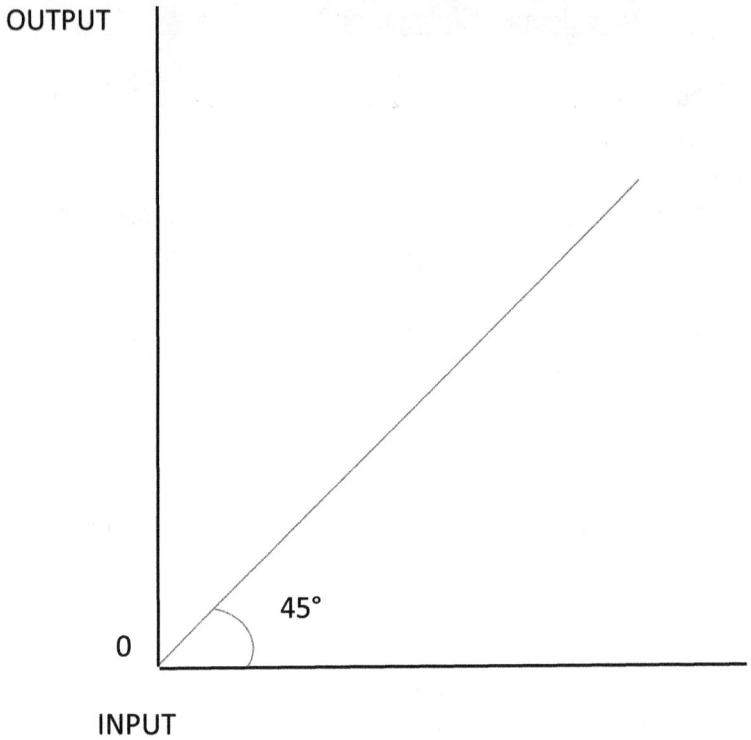

OUTPUT

45°

0

INPUT

Next, let's take the situation of Decreasing Returns to Scale. What does that look like? This is shown in the diagram below. Again, it is a technical difference to constant returns to scale, in that every increase unit increase in input causes less than a unit increase in output. Decreasing returns to scale is less efficient than constant returns to scale.

As can be seen in Figure 2, the line's slope is less than 45°.

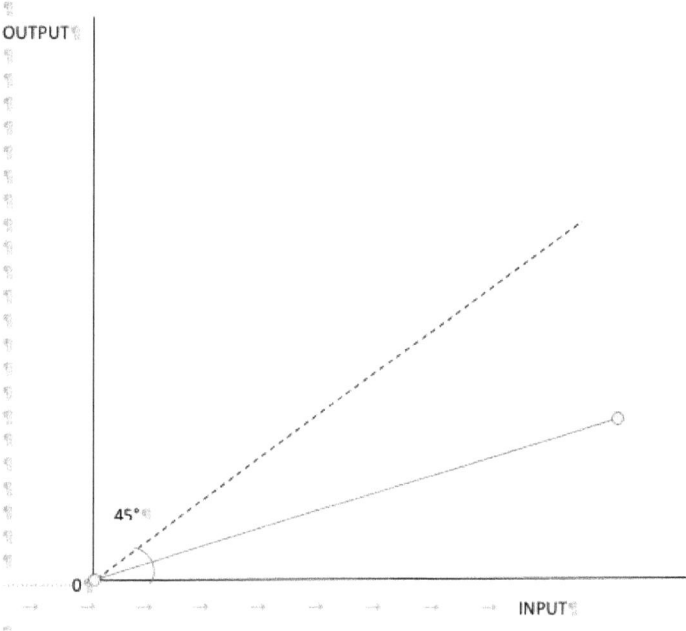

Figure two → → Decreasing Returns to Scale

OUTPUT

45°

0

INPUT

Finally, Increasing Returns to Scale. Figure three. This time the line slopes at more than 45°, as each unit of input causes more than more than one unit of output.

Figure three →   →   Increasing Returns to Scale

OUTPUT

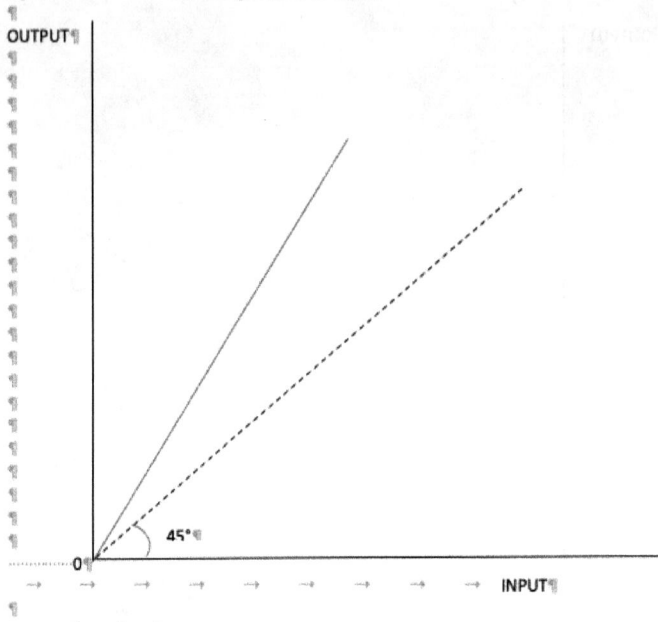

45°

0

INPUT

CHAPTER TWO

MOVING TO CURVED LINES

Obviously, in the real world, things do not move in straight lines. Furthermore, increasing and decreasing returns to scale are connected with the growth of the firm. All firms are operating at all times under either increasing and decreasing returns to scale.

Constant returns to scale? While there are vast areas of economic theory that are dependent on this concept, but in actual practice the aggregate value of constant returns to scale hardly exists. While there are many small firms operating under constant returns to scale, economists have found only a very small proportion of the *total value* of firms operate under constant returns to scale compared to the total value of firms operating under increasing or decreasing returns to scale. In other words, the total value of small firms is much less than the total value of large firms, even though small firms are much more numerous. (This is the result of the "Law of Distribution", that will be mentioned later. Sorry, there is nothing equal in this world).

In this chapter we will develop the economic theory of supply, we will get away from those straight lines and fixed quantities, and bring greater reality into this economic discussion.

The reason why we are doing this is to both move away from the straight lines of the previous chapters, and also the move into the price-quantity world from the straight quantity in – quantity out world. The ultimate reason will come apparent shortly.

When you get to curved lines, geometrically, there only three possible forms of (continuous) Supply in the price/quantity axis:
1. Concave up, called in economics Increasing Returns to Scale
2. Concave down, called in economics Decreasing Returns to Scale
3. Straight line. Called in economics Constant Returns to Scale

The above three possibilities are a geometric axiom. Like the axioms of Euclid. The above three types of curves can be shown in the form of the following diagrams:

Figure four   The concave up total product
curve, or increasing returns to scale

OUTPUT

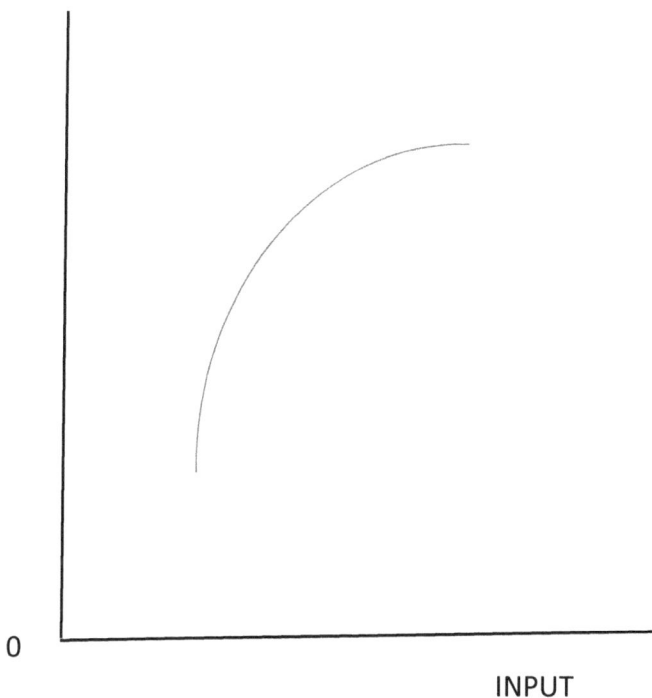

0

INPUT

As can be seen, the Increasing Returns to Scale supply curve is a curve that slopes upward at a faster rate than the rate of supply of inputs. Geometrically this is called concave up. The reason why this process is called increasing returns to scale is because the quantity of output increases at a faster rate in relative terms to the quantity of input.

Yes, these curve slopes are not completely accurate. At some point increasing returns to scale stops and tends towards constant returns to scale.

The second diagram has the opposite shaped curve, and is shown in Figure 5.

Figure Five   The concave down total product curve, or decreasing returns to scale

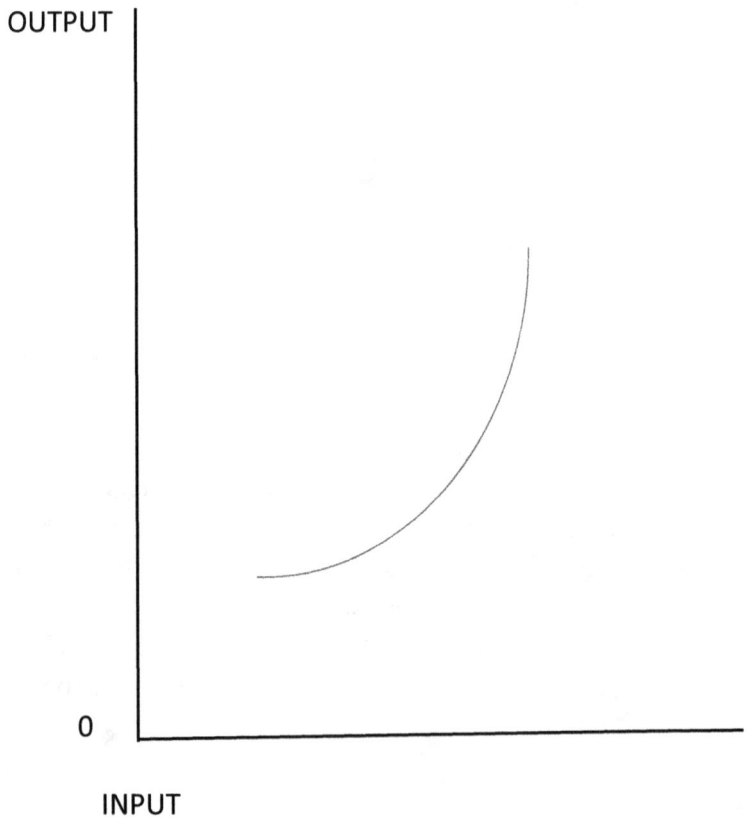

OUTPUT

0

INPUT

As can be seen, the decreasing returns to scale curve is a curve that slopes upwards at a slower rate. Geometrically it is called concave down. In economics it is called Decreasing Returns to Scale, as the quantity of output decreases at a faster rate in relation to the quantity of input.

The third figure is a Straight Line, or Constant Returns to Scale. This is shown in the diagram in Figure 6.

Figure Six   The straight-line total product
curve at 45°

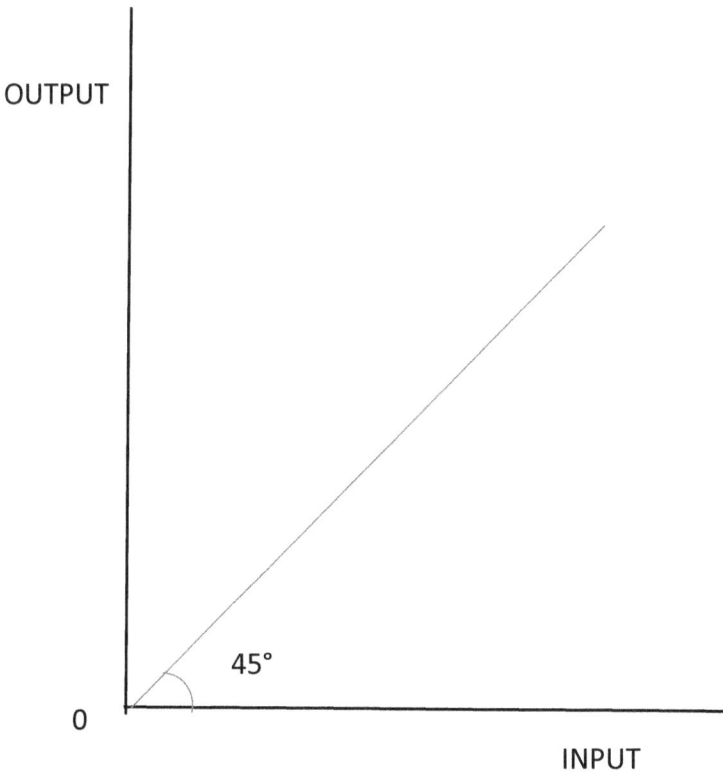

OUTPUT

45°

0

INPUT

Figure 6 shows that the quantity of output increases at the same rate as the quantity of input. This is a straight line, with a slope of 45°.

Looking at that line, it can be seen how artificial this construct is. A firm could easily fall off this trajectory and not return. In fact, so called "knife edge" economic theories, having the basic assumption of constant returns to scale, say this.

As an aside, it is amazing how much of economic theory has been built on the theory of constant returns to scale. This goes back historically to the beginnings of economic theory, but there are large areas of economics, such as general equilibrium theory, input-output theory, and indeed Marxist economic theory, that are dependent on the assumption of constant returns to scale.

From now on, this discussion gets slightly more complex, as it moves to greater realism. It will be seen later in this book, only two forms of production are possible, increasing returns to scale and decreasing returns to scale. However, decreasing returns to scale is very limited, and only happens when the firm ceases to operate under increasing returns to scale. This is when there is decreasing efficiency of management. Constant returns to scale is confined to very small firms, with fewer than two or three employees, such as small retailers. They cannot grow. While this area of small business is very numerous, it forms a very small proportion of the economy in aggregate value.

Research from taxation statistics in numerous countries show that the firms' total aggregate revenue, when plotted against the number of employees per firm, follows an inverse power law. Total aggregate revenue for small firms is very small compared to the total aggregate revenue for large firms. (Vijay Govindaragan, etc. 2019)

CHAPTER THREE

JOINING THE TOTAL PRODUCT CURVES

In order to obtain a better explanation of the production process in the real world, the Increasing Returns curve in Figure 6 and the Decreasing Returns Curve in Figure 7 are joined to form the so called 'S' curve. Also called a Sigmoid curve or a Logistic curve.

Yes, geometrically there are other possible combinations of the increasing returns, decreasing returns and constant returns to scale curves. But the other combinations are not economically realistic. Business economics has chosen the 'S' curve against any other possibilities. The universal assumption is that growth is slow at first, then it speeds up, and the it slows down. If you ask "Why should growth follow this pattern?". "Can't growth start out fast, the slow down, and then speed up again?", or alternatively "Can variable growth be interspersed with constant growth?", the answer is no. It is all to do with the cumulative rate of learning, and how it interacts with technology, production and output, and accumulated inefficiencies later in the growth phase. There has been a massive discussion on the 'S' curve. Most just explain it without question. A few give reasons why the alternatives don't exist. I good summary of this discussion is 'S-Curve Analysis' in "Strategy in 3D" by Greg Fisher, John E Warnock and Rene M. Bakker, 2020.

There is not enough space in this book to provide such a discussion. The reader will have to accept that the 'S' curve is all the happens in the business world. The other possibilities do not occur at all in the real world.

The next diagram, Figure 7, shows the joining of the Increasing Returns to Scale curve, in Figure 5 with the Decreasing Returns to Scale curve in Figure 6 to make the 'S' curve or the logistic curve.

Figure Seven   Joining the increasing returns
and decreasing returns to scale total product curves to
become a logistic curve

OUTPUT

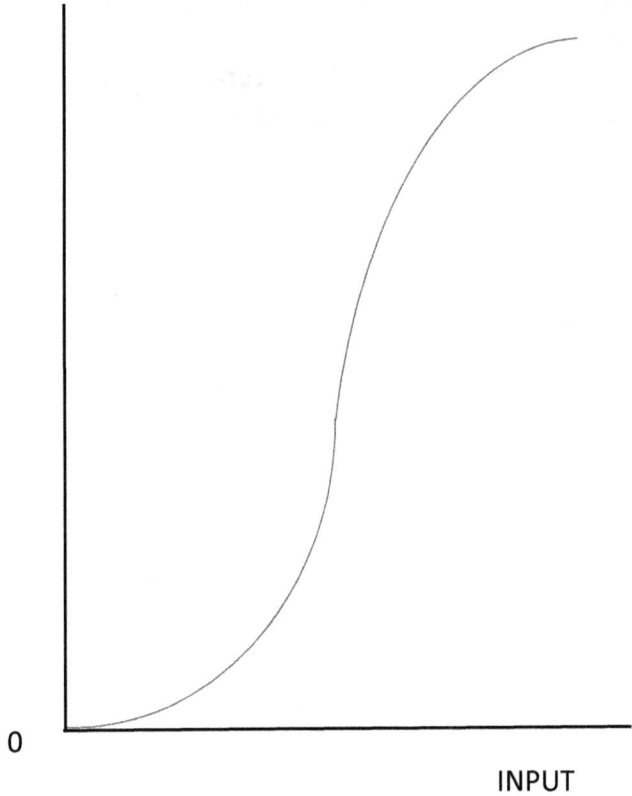

0

INPUT

In the above Figure seven, increasing returns to scale
comes first, and it is then joined by the decreasing
returns to scale curve. This is the so called 'S' curve.

Growth of the product starts at zero, and at first grows
gradually. As growth continues the growth rate

accelerates until it reaches a maximum. The curve is convex upwards. The curve then passes an inflexion point of constant returns to scale and growth begins to slow down. Growth becomes slower and slower, until growth ceases. This curve is concave downwards.

In economic usage, when the total product curve is concave upwards, the firm is operating under increasing returns to scale. When the total product curve is concave down the firm is operating under decreasing returns to scale.

While constant returns to scale is at the inflexion point, it is very small, and it can be seen on this diagram that the firm operates only in increasing returns to scale or decreasing returns to scale. Empirical work described in Chapter Fourteen shows that no large firms operate under constant returns to scale. The area of constant returns to scale is too unstable for large firms to operate in.

The only firms that can possibly operate under constant returns to scale are very small firms such as small retailers, with a couple of employees. As will be seen later, such firms are constrained to remain small and cannot expand. They rapidly reach a profit limit. Such very small firms are economically if not numerically a very small part of the aggregate economy.

CHAPTER FOUR

THE GROWTH OF THE FIRM

Let's start at the very basis of economics, going back to the start of Adam Smith's book *Wealth of Nations.* The growth of the firm. This can be described by the growth rate of the firm's total product. Take a simple model of the firm's inputs and outputs.

It is rare for the economics lecturer to describe how the supply curve is derived. If this is done, the process leads to major surprises. So, take a step back. Compare the growth of output in a simplified diagram with the quantity of input. There must be a whole range of inputs that go into that output. Let's narrow it down to one variable input, Labor, L, and assume away for now all other variable inputs. Assume the other major input, Capital, K, is constant. This is a very simple model, but it can be seen that other variable inputs would follow the same model.

Draw a diagram with total product, Q, on the 'y' axis and total input l/K on the 'x' axis. Now what would this relationship be? A straight line? While in the past, economist have been happy with this simplification, modern economic analysis has brought in an attempt at greater reality.

It has been well established experience that that the firm's economic growth usually takes the form of an 'S' curve. See Figure 8 above. Growth of product starts at zero, and at first it grows gradually. As growth continues, this growth in the rate of the product accelerates, until it reaches a maximum. This curve is concave upwards.

The curve then passes an inflection point and growth begins to slow down. The growth becomes slower and slower, until the curve is flat. This curve is concave downwards. Yes, this is a repeat of the latter part of Chapter Six, but the purpose is to introduce the economic concept of total product, and the Total Product Curve.

As can be seen in Figure 8, initially total product increases at a faster rate, and the curve is concave upwards. Then the rate of growth of the total product begins to slow, and the curve is concave downwards.

In economic usage, when the total product curve is concave upwards, the firm is operating under increasing returns to scale. This is when the rate of increase of total product output is faster than the rate of labor input. When the total product curve is concave down the firm is operating under decreasing returns to scale. This when the rate of increase of total product output is slower than the rate of increase of labor input. This is shown in Figure 8.

Figure Eight → → Increasing and Decreasing Returns to Scale of the Total Product Curve

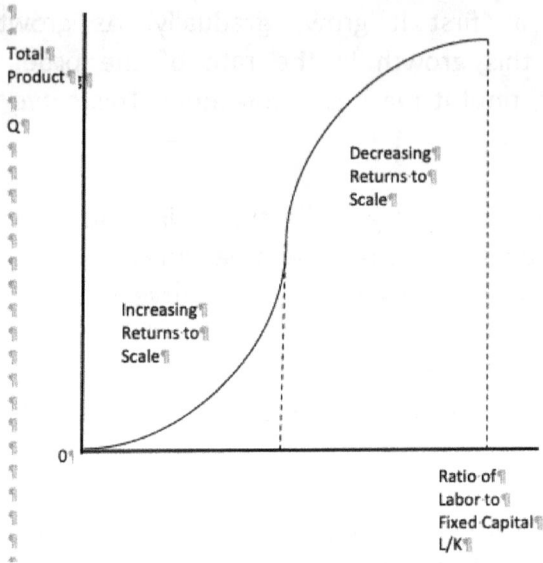

Total
Product

Q

Decreasing
Returns to
Scale

Increasing
Returns to
Scale

0

Ratio of
Labor to
Fixed Capital
L/K

Increasing returns to scale is the concave upward part of the curve where the rate of growth of output is more than the rate of growth of input.

Decreasing returns to scale is the concave downward part of the curve where the rate of growth of output is less than the rate of growth of input.

Constant returns to scale is at the inflection point. It is very small, and as can be seen the firm operates only in increasing returns to scale or decreasing returns to scale. There is no extended period where the firm operates under constant returns to scale.

In the real world it has been found that few if any large firms operate with constant returns to scale. Empirical research described in Chapter Thirteen describes that

25

all the firms analysed in the data set (firms quoted on the New York Stock Exchange) operate in either increasing returns to scale or decreasing returns to scale. No firm operates in precisely constant returns to scale, though many operate in the region but with increasing or decreasing returns to scale.

CHAPTER FIVE

DERIVING THE MARGINAL PRODUCT AND THE AVERAGE PRODUCT CURVES

From this Total Product curve can be derived the Marginal Product and the Average Product curves. The marginal product is the rate of growth of the Total Product curve. The average product is the total product at any point divided by the amount of labor input at that point. A marginal product can be found by the differential of the formula of the total product curve.

The Total Product curve can be more closely defined using a formula. Another name for the Logistic curve is the 'Sigmoid curve', or as it is commonly called, an 'S Curve'. The "y" axis is Total Product Q and the "x" axis is the ratio of Labor to Fixed Capital, L/K. Sigmoid curves are heavily used in business analysis to measure the growth rate of sales of a new product. It is also used in microbial biology to measure the growth rate of microbes in Petri dish. In a large number of applications, the concept is very useful.

A simple general formula of a Sigmoid curve is:

$$S(x) = \frac{1}{1 + e^{-x}} \; s$$

This is also called the logistic curve, or more commonly the 'S' shaped curve.

CHAPTER SIX

INTRODUCING PRICES AND COSTS

The process described so far does not involve prices and costs. Just the ratio of inputs to outputs. It is heavily used in the study of labor economics, where labor productivity is a measure of labor input to output, and increased labor productivity is regarded as a good thing.

It is true that you have to look at the productivity of all inputs, and there is a measure of Total Factor Productivity to measure this. If you go down this very interesting path for economists, you can study isoquants and the Cobb-Douglas Production function.

However, as I said, this is not an economics textbook, and we won't go in that direction. Instead it is necessary to go one step further, and introduce prices.

Why? I shall start with an example. Henry Ford designed and started manufacturing the Model-T Ford in 1910, and kept manufacturing the same Model-T, except for minor improvements, until 1929. Yes, labor productivity improved over this period, but not by much. They started with the assembly line, and while at the start a worker inserted four bolts in a wheel, at the end he only inserted one. There was increasing division of labor, and increasing labor productivity thereby. The speed of production and labor productivity in this period more than doubled.

However, the cost of production decreased ten times. In 1910 the cost of production per car was around $250, but by 1929, the cost of production was less than $25 per car.

Was this due to increased labor productivity? In this period, labor productivity perhaps doubled, at most. Capital productivity also increased. But what brought about this major fall in costs was a major fall in the price of inputs, although wage costs actually increased. Suppliers were continuously forced to drop their prices. The main reason for the major fall in the cost of the Model-T was a fall in their input prices.

There is a lesson here for the intending entrepreneur. While measures of physical productivity are important, and you should always try to improve them; it is the costs of the other inputs that are vastly more important. You should be always trying to reduce these in a continuous cycle.

So, what are increasing returns to scale, constant returns to scale and decreasing returns to scale, in terms of prices?

When students are taught economics, they are soon taught the 'supply demand model' in the form of a diagram, with price on the vertical axis and the quantity on the horizontal axis. We shall use that diagram here, but for the moment, we won't look at demand. We are only interested in supply and the price of supply.

There is a connection between the physical supply diagrams and the following diagrams with a price axis, but we need not waste space making this connection. Again we are not an economics textbook.....(Oh, no? This is already mind-numbingly boring! But dear reader, as you will soon find, necessary.) If you want more details I suggest that you open a suitable Microeconomics textbook. (See the index at the back for Swann and McEachern (2006) and Varian (2010))

Figure nine shows a very simple straight-line diagram of price on the vertical axis and quantity on the horizontal axis for an increasing returns to scale supply line. Note that from now on, quantities are not on both axes, but price is on one axis.

PRICE

Negatively sloped
Supply line

0

QUANTITY

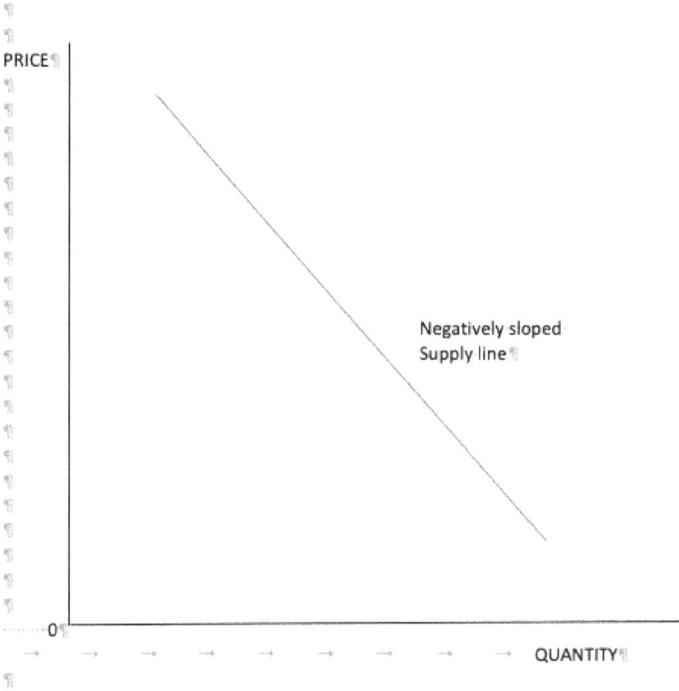

As can be seen above, the Supply line in terms of prices and quantities has a negative slope, the opposite slope to the increasing returns to scale of physical output of Figure three. If these goods are being manufactured, as output increases the cost of manufacture falls.

Now this does not happen all the time. In the next figure, Figure 10, you can see that the line is horizontal. As quantity sold increases the cost of production remains the same.

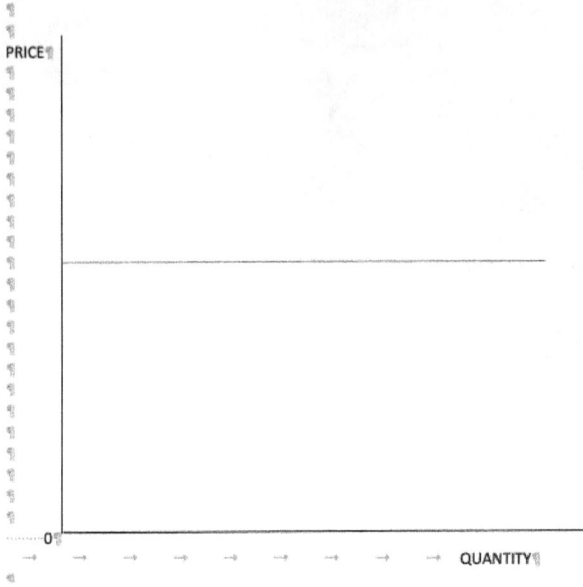

Figure ten → ⋯∘ → Constant returns to scale supply line

PRICE

0

QUANTITY

In the next figure, Figure eleven, the line has a positive slope. As quantity sold increases the cost of production increases. This is called decreasing returns to scale.

Note that when the Supply line in the price/quantity axis has a negative slope, it is said to have increasing returns to scale. When the Supply line in the price/quantity axis has a positive slope, it is said to have a decreasing returns to scale.

Figure eleven → → Decreasing returns to scale supply line

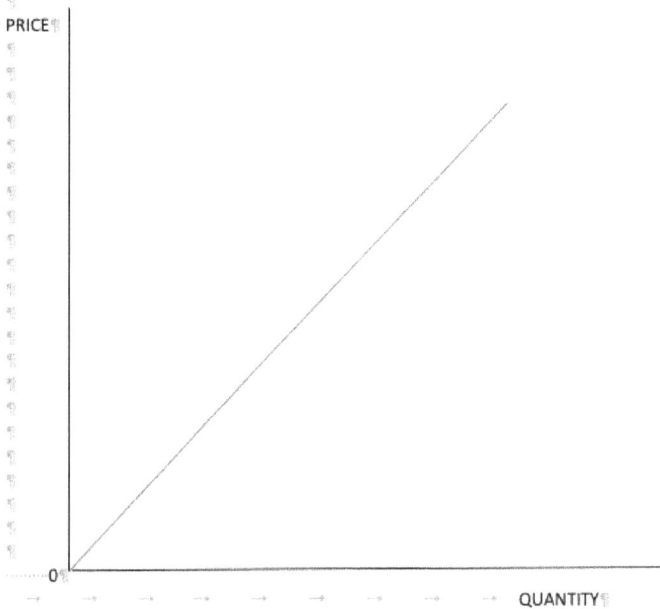

PRICE

0

QUANTITY

As said earlier, changes in physical productivity, while interesting to the economist, are not really relevant in the real world. I referred to Henry Ford's Model-T, where labor productivity doubled over 20 years, while cost of production fell to one tenth of what it was at the start. Business men and women are only partly interested in labor productivity, but they are mainly interested in costs, especially marginal costs.

So how do you insert costs into those product curves? This is shown in the following Figure 12.

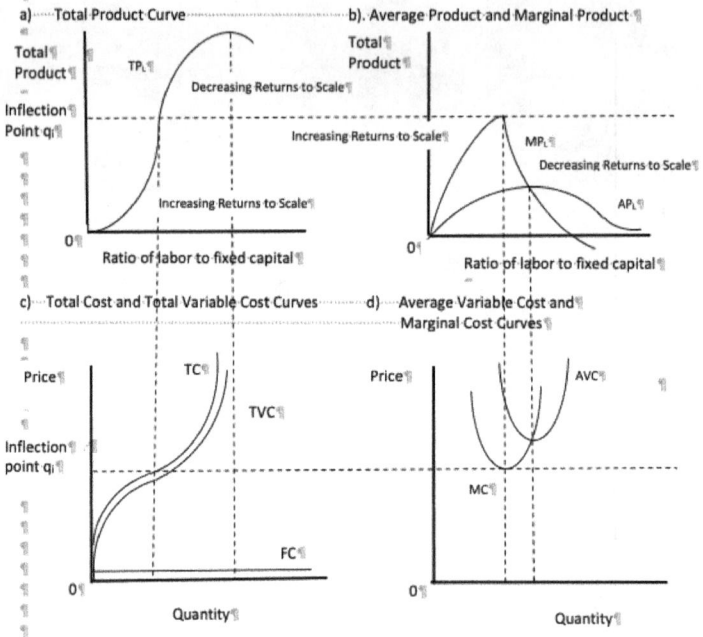

Figure twelve → → Four standard charts converting quantities to prices

a) Total Product Curve .... b). Average Product and Marginal Product

a) Total Product Curve

Total Product

TP

Decreasing Returns to Scale

Inflection Point q_i

Increasing Returns to Scale

0

Ratio of labor to fixed capital

b). Average Product and Marginal Product

Total Product

Increasing Returns to Scale

MP

Decreasing Returns to Scale

APL

0

Ratio of labor to fixed capital

c) Total Cost and Total Variable Cost Curves .... **d) Average Variable Cost and Marginal Cost Curves**

Price

TC

TVC

Inflection point q_i

FC

0

Quantity

Price

AVC

MC

0

Quantity

Chart (a) shows the Sigmoid shape of the growth of Total Product.

Chart (b) shows the marginal product and average product curves derived from the total product curve. The first part of the marginal product curve is concave down, and thus is increasing returns to scale. The second part of the marginal product curve from the inflection point onwards is concave up and decreasing returns to scale. Dividing the total product by total labor gives the curved average product curve passes through the peak of the average product curve., rising to a peak but never falling to zero.

35

This average product curve with the denominator being labor is the measure of labor productivity, which reaches a peak and then declines. It is interesting to note that while the firm continues to operate under increasing returns to scale labor productivity can never decline. Declining labor productivity is a sign of declining returns to scale.

Chart (c) introduces costs, which are divided into two parts, fixed costs and variable cost. Total fixed costs is the flat line a the bottom. Total variable costs is the curved line rising from zero, and its shape reflects the total product curve at the top. Total costs are the total variable costs plus unit fixed costs, so it parallels the total variable cost line.

Chart (d) demonstrates the relationship between Marginal Cost and Marginal Product, when you add costs from Chart (c) to marginal product and average product. The curves now go in the opposite directions. Marginal cost turns upwards at the inflection point and passes through minimum average variable cost.

As is shown,

$$MC = \frac{\$W}{MP}$$

$$AVC = \frac{\$W}{AP}$$

Where $W is the monetary value of wages (it could be any unit cost).

Thus, there is a direct relationship between marginal product and marginal cost.

Also, average variable *cost* is connected to total costs and total product. This leads to average variable costs and marginal costs. See the formulae above.

Marginal costs are a very important concept. Not only does the firm depend on the operation of marginal costs, but marginal costs are the equivalent to the supply function of the firm, and through that to the concepts of increasing returns to scale, constant returns to scale and decreasing returns to scale in money terms. And that is what it is all about. How a firm operates all depends on the shape of its marginal cost curve. Add in the demand curve (described later) and (at least theoretically) you have the complete story of how a firm works. If you want to maximise the potential returns from your firm, you have to set the firm's operations to maximise the use of the criteria which will be described. These are, increasing returns to scale and a flat demand curve.

CHAPTER SEVEN

PROOF THAT THE MARGINAL COST CURVE IS THE SAME AS THE SUPPLY CURVE

Most text books ignore this proof. They gradually merge Demand with Marginal Cost without an explanation.

The following is a proof:

When the firms are competitive i.e. they act as a price taker, they take their supply decisions by maximizing the profits .

Taking price p as given:

Max q $pq - C(q)$

where q is the quantity and $C(q)$ is the cost function of the firm.

The solution to the above problem is known as the supply at price p. The solution can vary with price p.

Under standard assumptions on cost functions such as: it is increasing, continuously differentiable and strictly convex, and satisfy

Lim $q \to 0$ $C'(q) = 0$

and

$$\lim q \to \infty \; C'(q) = \infty$$

the solution to the profit maximization problem (supply) will satisfy:

$$p = C'(q)$$

So, (q,p) such that $p = C'(q)$ is the supply curve, and $(q, C'(q))$ is the marginal cost curve.

But since $p = C'(q)$, they are the same. The supply curve is the same as the marginal cost curve.

CHAPTER EIGHT

DEMAND AND MARGINAL REVENUE

Up to this point, we have not mentioned Demand. We have concentrated solely on Supply. This is contrary to normal economics teaching that puts a priority on Demand, and tends to place Supply as secondary. The concentration of this book is on Supply. Yes, the consideration of Demand is important to intending entrepreneurs, especially consideration of the slope of the potential demand curve. As you will see, the flatter the demand curve the better. But if you don't thoroughly understand the concept of Supply initially, you will get nowhere, regardless of the demand for your product.

So, what is Demand? It is the quantity sold at a given price.

The normal assumption of economics is that is price falls the quantity sold increases. This is not the invariable situation however. A common situation is inelastic demand, where increasing price does not increase the quantity sold. This describes the market for land. No more land is manufactured. Increasing the price for land does not increase the quantity of land available to be sold. The demand for land is aid to be "inelastic". Very occasionally, increases in price cause increasing demand. This is the case of certain luxury goods, or a few employment markets, where increased wages decrease demand. These are called Giffen Goods. But in general, markets are "well behaved", where reduced prices lead to a steady increase in prices.

In the following diagram, Figure thirteen, where the axes Price and Quantity, the Demand curve is shown to be Downward sloping.

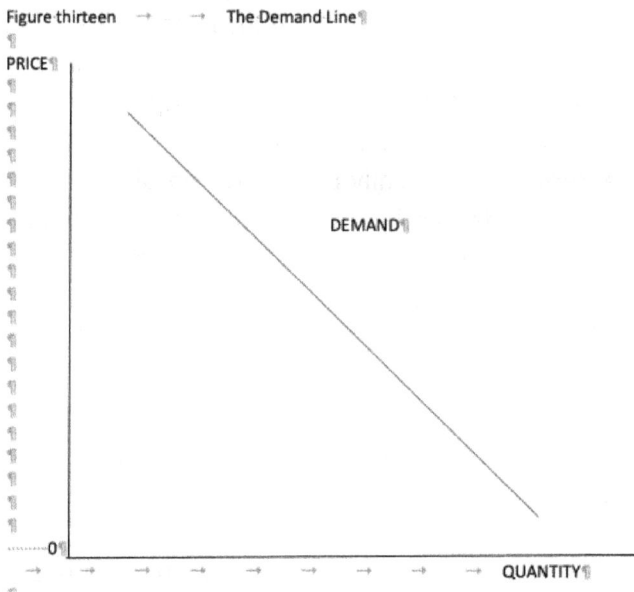

Figure thirteen → → The Demand Line

PRICE

DEMAND

0

QUANTITY

Now the Demand line is also called the Average Revenue line. Revenue at any point divided by Quantity is Price. Price at any point is therefore Average Revenue. This is shown in the next diagram, Figure 12.

Why is demand the same as average revenue? Simple. The demand line shows the quantity Q sold at price P. It is not necessarily a straight line. It could be a curve. But the line is a locus of P and Q. P = f(Q).

Now revenue R is P x Q at any point.

Average revenue is $\frac{R}{Q}$

$$\frac{R}{Q.} = \frac{P \times Q}{Q}$$

Thus $\qquad \frac{R}{Q} = P$

Figure fourteen $\quad\rightarrow\quad\rightarrow$ The average revenue line

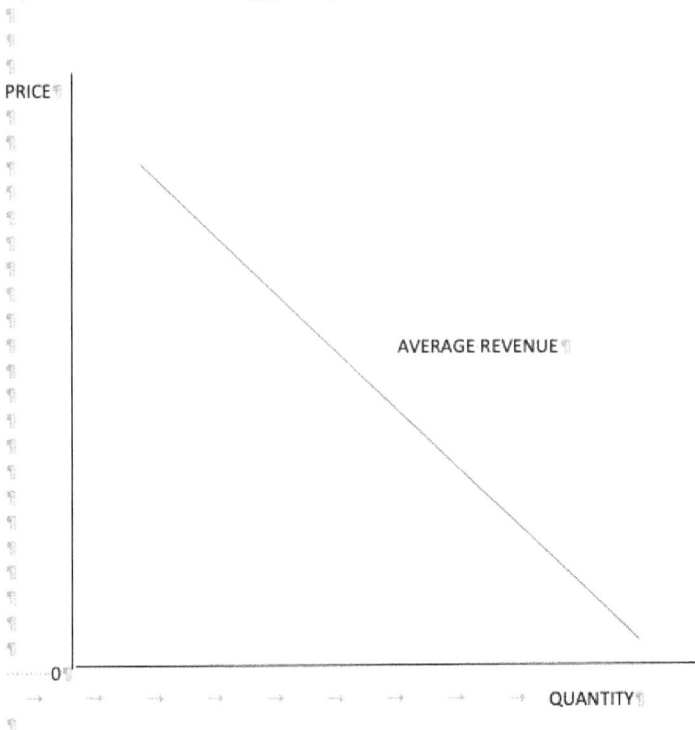

PRICE

AVERAGE REVENUE

0

QUANTITY

As P is demand, average revenue is the same as Demand

From here we make our way to the concept of Supply and Demand. This is where Supply crosses Demand, and the equilibrium price is at this point.

Figure fifteen → → The standard supply and demand diagram

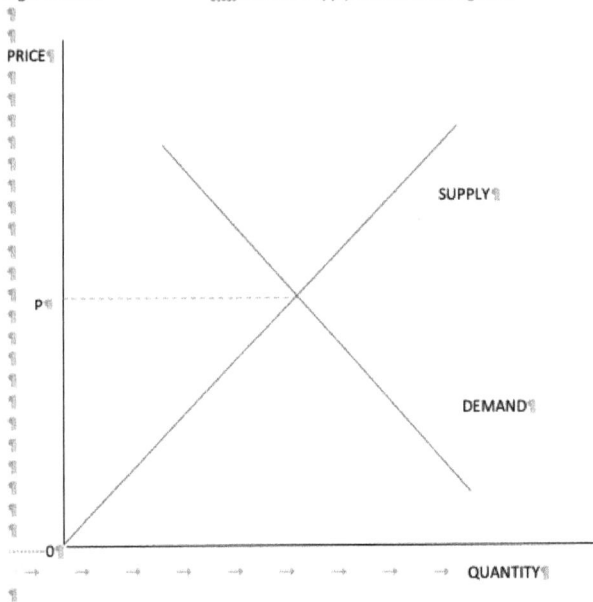

The equilibrium price is P.

The above is the standard supply/demand diagram, as taught to economics students everywhere. Economics lectures like to say when they draw these lines on the board "Now you are economists. Remember, price is not directly related to costs, but to supply and demand." (Yes, supply is marginal cost, but this is different from average cost.)

The supply line need not always be upward sloping. As will be explained in forthcoming chapters, the supply/marginal cost line is only upward sloping when the firm is operating under decreasing returns to scale. When the firm is operating under increasing returns to scale the line is downward sloping.

With a downward sloping demand/average revenue line, the marginal revenue line starts at the same point on the 'y' axis and is also downward sloping, but it is steeper and inside the average revenue line. This is because

1. When the value of the average revenue is zero, the value of the marginal revenue is zero.
2. With a downward sloping average revenue line, the marginal revenue line is below the average revenue line, and when the average revenue line has a positive slope the marginal revenue line is above the average revenue line. However, the latter situation in practice of average revenue increasing with volume is hardly ever likely to occur.

This is shown in the next diagram, Figure 16.

Figure sixteen → The relationship between average revenue and marginal revenue

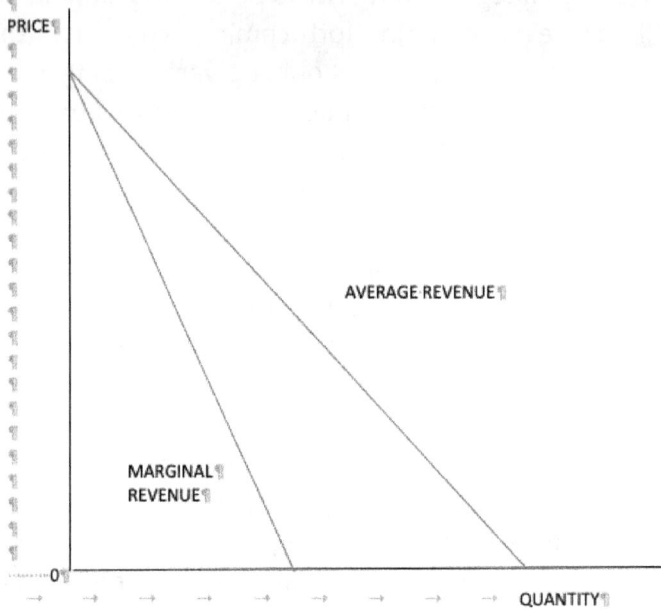

It can be shown that when average revenue and marginal revenue are straight lines, the marginal revenue line reaches the 'x' axis at half the distance from the origin as the average revenue line. This proof is shown in Appendix 1.

CHAPTER NINE

THE RELATIONSHIP OF PROFIT TO MARGINAL COST, MARGINAL REVENUE AND AVERAGE REVENUE

Remember that marginal cost is equivalent to Supply, and average revenue is equivalent to Demand. (Students at this point get confused and sometimes equate marginal revenue to Demand. It is not.)

The following diagram, Figure 17, shows marginal revenue, average revenue and a curved marginal cost. This diagram is central to what is happening and is very important.

PRICE

Decreasing returns tor scale

Increasing returns to scale

AVERAGE REVENUE
OR DEMAND

MARGINAL
COST OR
SUPPLY

MARGINAL
REVENUE

0

QUANTITY

The declining component of the curved marginal costs identifies increasing returns to scale. The increasing component of the marginal cost curve identifies increasing returns to scale.

CHAPTER TEN

PROFIT

Now we are getting to the purpose of this book. Making a profit. Now the average person would say, "That's simple. Profit is the difference between sales revenue and costs." Hmmmm...It is not quite that simple, I am sorry to say. For your firm to survive and prosper, you need a better understanding regarding the relationship between profits and revenue. There is not a constant relationship. *High revenues may reduce profits*. Profits go up and down in a manner that is mysterious to the uninitiated.

So, I shall start by stating that profits are maximised when marginal revenue equals marginal costs. Huh? I shall explain.

We have already explained what both marginal revenue and marginal cost is. Vital pieces of information for the entrepreneur. (But how many so-called CEO's know this necessary information?) You are already ahead of the curve, after all those boring diagrams.

From this, as already been described, you can (and must) work out the marginal revenue for your product. The relationship between falling prices and increased sales. Marginal revenue is the change in revenue divided by the change in the number of goods sold. (See Appendix 2). It is not just a theoretical requirement.

Your firm's survival depends on this knowledge. Maybe you think your firm can sell at a constant price forever. Not even Microsoft can do that. Microsoft cuts prices, has discounts, to increase sales.

You should also have a detailed knowledge of costs. Fixed costs and variable costs. Variable costs will vary with output. Add fixed costs and variable costs to obtain total costs at a point in time, or more precisely – total costs at each level of output. As fixed costs are unchanging, total costs will decrease with increasing output.

But only up to a certain point. Then it is the unfortunate fate of all firms. They reach a point of decreasing efficiency and increasing variable costs, and then *costs increase with increasing output.*

Marginal costs are derived from total costs (not average costs). Marginal costs are the <u>change</u> in total costs when output increases. Again, this method has already been described, and relationship between total cost and marginal cost has already been described. Marginal cost and marginal revenue lines are shown in Figure 18.

The proof for profit maximising is in Appendix 3. Precisely, a firm's profits are at a maximum when Marginal Revenue equals Marginal Cost.

In terms of the formula in Appendix 2, when

$$\Delta R / \Delta q = p\{1 + \frac{q\Delta p}{\Delta q}\} = \Delta c$$

where c is cost of the unit with price p.

This is shown in Figure 18.

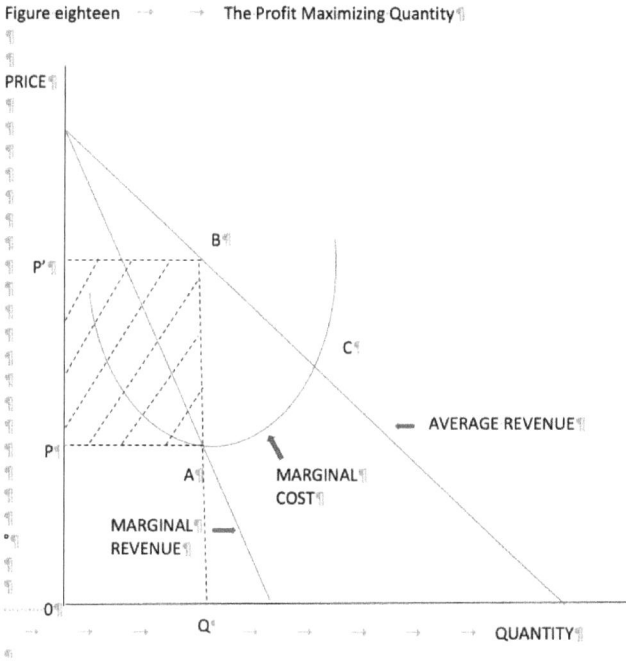

Maximum profit is the shaded area P P' B A. Profit maximising Q is where the marginal cost line crosses the marginal revenue line.

CHAPTER ELEVEN

THE DOWNWARD SLOPING AND UPWARD SLOPING SUPPLY CURVES

Now we are getting to the point of this theoretical exercise. What is it? You have set up your firm, and think prices are set by 'supply and demand'. Nope. Supply and demand is a very useful theoretical construct to wean people from an even worse belief, that prices are cost plus a margin, or an even worse belief, prevalent in the 19th century, the labor theory of value (prices are equivalent to labor input). Yes, prices are set by market demand, but not exactly as in the 'supply demand' diagram in Figure 1. For your firm to prosper and grow, you must grasp the concept of increasing returns to scale and pricing along the demand line.

So back to Figures seventeen and eighteen. In Figure seventeen we have three things, a supply or marginal revenue line, a demand line and a marginal revenue line. The major difference between this diagram and normal theory is that the demand or marginal cost line stops at the demand line, at point C. Why? Because at this point profits cease. If the supplier supplies products beyond the demand line he will make a loss. So, there is no incentive to supply goods beyond the demand line.

Why is the supplier making a loss? If the line AB is pushed to the right, it can be seen that the size of the profit, ABP'P gets smaller. When the line AB reaches C,

where the supply line reaches the demand line, profit is
zero.

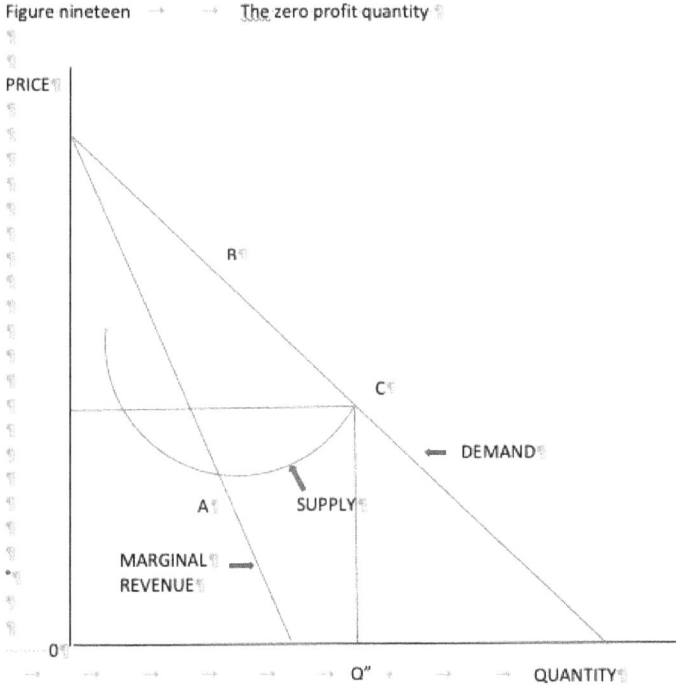

Figure nineteen   →   The zero profit quantity

What happens when the lines P'A and PB in Figure 19
extend out to point C on the demand line? They move
closer together until the size of the total profit
quadrangle P'ABP becomes zero. In other words, at
quantity Q'', when the supply curve crosses the demand
curve, total profit is zero. In the standard
Supply/Demand cross curve, Figure fifteen, the so-
called equilibrium price is when total profit is zero.

Saying the system is in equilibrium when total profit is
zero maybe theoretically correct, but it is not very
useful. Or to put it another way, when the firm is profit

maximising it is not in equilibrium! Economic theory is replete with these contradictions. It is only in equilibrium when its profit is zero!

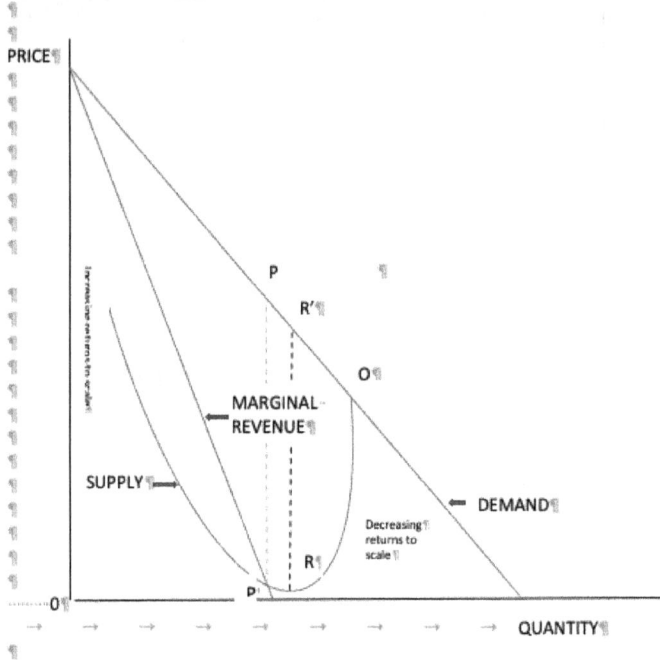

Figure twenty → The maximum unit profit

In Figure twenty, the maximum total profit is at PP' (marginal revenue equals marginal cost). There is zero profit at O, when the supply curve crosses the demand line, and the price of goods that can be supplied exceeds the price that can be paid.

RR' is the unit profit at constant returns to scale.

PP>RR' when the firm is operating under increasing returns to scale.

PP=RR' when the frim operates under constant returns to scale.
PP<RR' when the firm operates under decreasing returns to scale.

A major benefit of operating under increasing returns to scale is that it is unlikely to make zero profits. (It can, if the supply curve is very close to the demand curve, and it crosses at some point). But in the real world, most firms operate first under increasing returns to scale far below the demand line.

With the geometry of a downward sloping demand curve, the decreasing returns to scale component of the supply curve is likely to be shorter than the increasing returns to scale component, that starts when the firm commences operations in the top left-hand corner. Furthermore, if the firm increases production under decreasing returns to scale, the firm eventually will cease making a profit.

Thus, it is preferable for the firm to remain in the increasing returns to scale production area. As long as the firm continues to operate under increasing returns to scale it is unlikely to cease making profits, and thus go out of business. Operating under decreasing returns to scale, the firm is in the area of decreasing unit and total profits, leading to zero profits.

That begs the question, how does one remain in the area of increasing returns to scale? It is simple for those who know how. All it takes in a simple formula. This will be described in the next chapter.

This is nearly the end of the chapters on economic theory. If the reader has got this far, he has greater understanding of the economic forces affecting the firm. He is far ahead than the vast majority of business people who, if they get into trouble they depend on advice of accountants, MBA's and McKinsey. (Don't).

CHAPTER TWELVE

ESTIMATING RETURNS TO SCALE
FOR YOUR FIRM

I have written a book on this subject *Increasing Returns to Scale: A Simple Way to Make Good investments and Bad investments when Investing in Company Shares*. Since the book was published in 2013 a number of readers have, they have told me, made substantial gains from using this book. A couple have even set up funds, and from all accounts are budding Warren Buffets!

The book tells how to detect those listed companies that are operating under increasing returns to scale, and those who are not. Those firms that operate under increasing returns to scale make increasing profits, and are a safe investment. Those firms that operate under decreasing returns to scale make decreasing profits, and may even go bust.

The downside with this method is that it involves a lot of hard work grinding out the figures.

For the reader of this book, that hard work is not necessary. You are dealing with only one firm. Your own. You can set up processes. You can then say "I won't hire so many people. I won't invest that amount unless I can be guaranteed that amount of sales. What has happened to sales? It should be this amount. Is somebody filtering off a part of the revenue?" The beauty of this method is that that everything fits together. If something does not work as it should, you can easily spot it. If you are going off the rails, you can get back on. Like certain sophisticated audit systems, you can spot what should not happen, and correct it. At all times, the firm can and must remain in the area of increasing returns to scale.

So how does this method work?

The methodology depends on the Cobb-Douglas Production function.

$$Y = DK^{\alpha}L^{\beta}$$

Where   Y = the firm's revenue in that year
                K = the firm's value of capital in that

year

                L = the firm's labor cost in that year
                D is a fixed coefficient
                α = the relative efficiency of capital of

the firm

                β = the relative efficiency of labor of the

firm

                $\alpha + \beta$ = the measure of returns to scale
                If $\alpha > 0$ the revenue elasticity of expenditure for capital expenditure is positive. This means that for every additional dollar invested in capital, revenue increases by the same amount of dollars.
                If $\alpha < 0$ the   revenue   elasticity   of expenditure for capital expenditure is negative. This

means that for every additional dollar invested capital, revenue decreases by the same amount of dollars.

If $\beta > 0$ the revenue elasticity of expenditure for labor expenditure is positive. This means that for every additional dollar invested spent on labor, revenue increases by the same amount of dollars.

If $\beta < 0$ the revenue elasticity of expenditure for labor expenditure is negative. This means that for every additional dollar spent on labor, revenue decreases by the same amount of dollars.

Data is extracted for two successive years, marked 1 and 2.

The above two functions 1 and 2 are then logged.

Assuming α and β are unchanged over the two following years, then:

$$\alpha = \frac{\ln L_2 \ln Y_1 - \ln L_1 \ln Y_2}{\ln L_2 \ln K_1 - \ln L_1 \ln K_2}$$

$$\beta = \frac{\ln Y_1 - \alpha \ln k_1}{\ln L_1}$$

or

$$\beta = \frac{\ln Y_2 - \alpha \ln k_2}{\ln L_2}$$

α is the relative efficiency of capital expenditure
β is the relative efficiency of labor
L is the quantity of labor, K is the quantity of capital, and Y is income in the respective periods 1 and 2.

For your own firm, this information comes straight out of your own accounts.

Investment Data. If you have an Investment fund. For the US, I used the SEC 10-K site for financial data. Dry but informative. Company Annual Reports are difficult to use, and often try to hide important information.

I tested using statistical regression whether $\alpha_1 = \alpha_2$ and $\beta_1 = \beta_2$. I found that they equalled within a 95% confidence interval.

In conclusion, using this empirical method, I have found that around half the large quoted firms in the USA operated under increasing returns to scale, and a much higher proportion of smaller quoted firms operated under increasing returns to scale. My untested inference is that nearly all small un-quoted firms above the size of "small business" operate under increasing returns to scale. That would be an objective for a very important empirical investigation.

Table 1   Estimation of Increasing and Decreasing Returns to Scale for selected companies

Company name	Y1 Income Year1	K1 Capital Year1	L1 Wages Year1	Y2 Income Year2	K2 Capital Year2	L2 Wages Year2	α	β	$\alpha+\beta$ Returns to Scale
American Express	33776	15314	6597	34932	15337	6171	1.22	-0.47	0.748
Apple	65225	75183	7299	10824	11637	10028	3.08	-2.6434	0.4382
BP	375765	146323	12327	379136	151457	13117	1.72	-0.8127	0.9102
Caterpillar	2693	34742	416	2783	35138	427	0.03	1.2428	1.2841
Chevron	253706	209474	26394	241909	232982	27294	-1.34	2.8375	1.4953
Coca Cola	46542	79974	28327	48017	86174	28964	0.15	0.8753	1.0295
Disney	36149	63117	30452	38063	69206	31337	0.36	0.6249	0.9907
Du Pont	36144	51499	29142	35310	49859	32252	0.91	0.0602	0.9705
General Electric	147288	718189	54185	147359	685328	53912	-0.14	1.2745	1.1267
General Motors	150276	144603	130386	152256	149422	140236	1.48	-0.49	0.9989
IBM	127245	116433	55533	104507	119213	53122	0.95	0.0352	0.9949
Intel	53999	71119	36262	53441	84351	28395	0.56	0.4413	1.0019
JP Morgan Chase	97031	2359141	30585	96606	2415689	30810	0.72	0.0856	0.8063
Microsoft	73723	121271	38237	77849	142431	30836	0.70	0.2745	0.9845
Pepsi	66504	72882	31593	65492	74638	31291	-0.14	1.23	1.0837
Shell	47017	34525	14335	46715	36032	14616	-1.95	3.96	2.0439

The attached is a snippet from my book *"Increasing Returns to Scale"*. This table gives a calculated measure of increasing and decreasing returns to scale for selected companies in the year 2013. I might add that many have profited from using this simple technique.

Alpha is the returns to scale for capital, and beta is the returns to scale for labor. Added together, they are the total returns to scale for the company. If the individual amounts or the total are above one, then that means increasing returns to scale for that variable. If the amount is less than one, that means decreasing returns to scale for that variable. This table was for the year 2013. Things could have changed since then, so I don't advise using the table to make investment. I suggest that you buy the book and use it to make your own calculations.

The above is a summary of the method you can use for making profitable investments. But you have a single business that you want to keep track off, and keep in increasing returns to scale. What methodology shall you use?

I suggest that you use the following simple methodology.

Step 1. Divide your firm's accounting records into two periods. These periods need not be years, even though a year is convenient if you do not want to upset the accountants! Shorter periods may be useful, but capital expenditure can be "lumpy".

Step 2. Identify the number of employees in each period, and call them L_1 and L_2. You can use the wage bill in each period, but remember to adjust for inflation/wage rises.

Step 2. Identify the expenditure on capital items in each period. I could specify "productive" capital expenditure, but that is not necessary. If you spend on wood panelled offices, expensive cars and pile carpets, it will come out in the wash (badly). Again adjust for inflation. These are items K! and K2.

Step 3. Sales in each period, Y1 and Y2. Again adjust for inflation.

Apply the formulae

$$\alpha = \frac{\ln L_2 \ln Y_1 - \ln L_1 \ln Y_2}{\ln L_2 \ln K_1 - \ln L_1 \ln K_2}$$

$$\beta = \frac{\ln Y_1 - \alpha \ln k_1}{\ln L_1}$$

or

$$\beta = \frac{\ln Y_2 - \alpha \ln k_2}{\ln L_2}$$

If $\alpha + \beta > 0$ your firm is operating under increasing returns to scale, and you should be happy. If not, look at the values of each of α and β and adjust these values so as to obtain increasing returns to scale. You are effectively reverse engineering your firm. After some refiguring, you should get a desired outcome – target figures for capital and labour, or total revenue.

If either α or β are negative it is a worry. You must curb employee growth or capital expenditure until this figure is positive. These are warning signals. Or alternatively specify a desired increase in sales in the next period, or else.....!

It is usually quite simple to curb growth in these items. What was the "non-quality/non profitable" growth area in these items? Drill down to the source. Somebody has been pressing to increase these items. Why? Don't let it happen again.

CHAPTER THIRTEEN

DEMAND

Hitherto fore we have concentrated on supply and the structure of the firm. Specifically, we have recommended that the firm should operate under increasing returns to scale, a measure that is derived from the shape of the marginal cost/ supply curve. This advice is generally neglected, and economic life would be far better if the requirement to take special note of the direction of the supply/marginal cost curve was remembered and acted upon.

However, the firm also operates in a market. *After* the firm has been set up and starts producing goods and services, and remember the word I have used "after", attention should be turned to the subject of Demand.

What is "Demand"? The economic definition of demand is the quantity of a good that would be purchased by a consumer at a specific price.

In most circumstances, an increased quantity will be demanded as the price falls. Demand is a behavioural activity. It is heavily dependent on human behaviour.

Figure twenty-one shows a downward sloping demand line. This is so-called market demand. Notionally if a firm sells only a small quantity of a product, it can charge a high price per unit. As the firm increases production and sales, each increase in sales can be sold on the market at only a lower price.

Figure twenty-one → → A downward sloping demand line

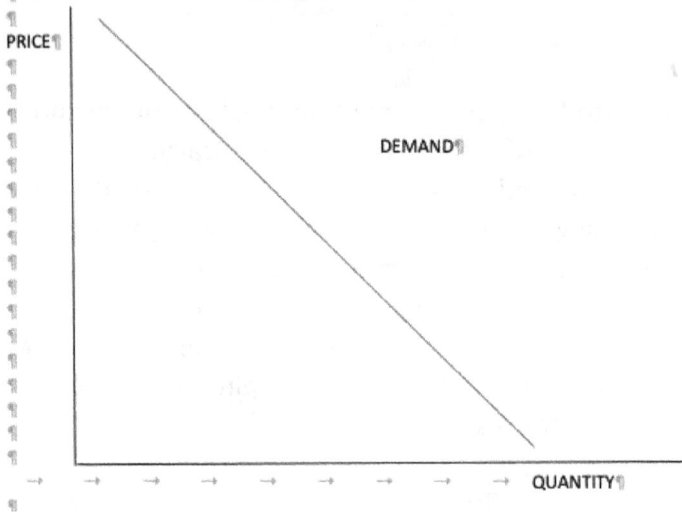

PRICE

DEMAND

QUANTITY

What happens to revenue? It could continue to increase or decrease. If price declines at a slower rate than the increase in quantity sold, revenue continues to increase. If price declines at a faster rate than the increase in quantity, revenue declines. This is the question of so-called elasticity. I don't want to confuse the reader with questions of elasticity. If you reach the above situation, hire a good economist.

CHAPTER FOURTEEN

THE OPTIMUM SALES STRATEGY – A FLAT DEMAND CURVE

Microsoft is supposed to have a flat demand curve. Thus, it is supposed that the demand for Microsoft products at their offer price is supposed to be almost infinite. It can sell unlimited quantities of its products at a fixed price. In actual fact, that is not technically true. Microsoft has no control over the demand for its products. That is under control of the market, not Microsoft. (In practice, Microsoft can shift the demand curve for its products to the right through a marketing campaign, but we won't go into that).

So, what is this flat curve? It is effectively a supply curve. The price Microsoft sells its good onto the market that is totally under control of Microsoft.

If you look back at Figure fifteen you will see a downward sloping demand line and an upward sloping supply line. It is supposed that a firm will increase the quantity of its product supplied to the market as the price goes up.

Figure twenty-two shows a flattened demand/supply curve hitting the downward sloping demand curve.

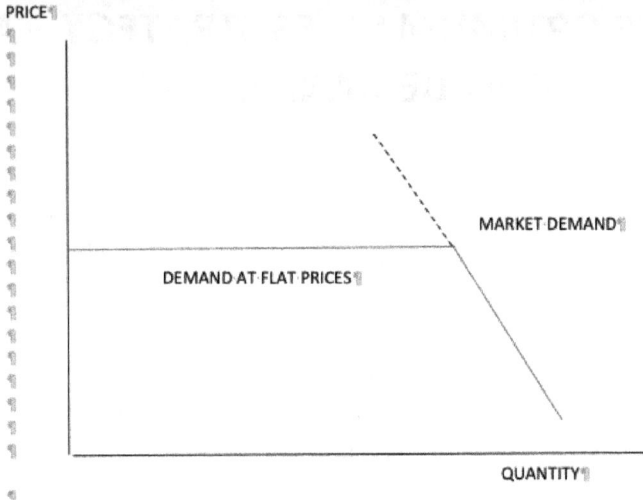

Figure Twenty-two → → Flat prices and the limit of the market

PRICE

MARKET DEMAND

DEMAND AT FLAT PRICES

QUANTITY

As can be seen, the firm that sells at a constant price thinks that it has infinite demand. Suddenly it hits market demand, and it can only increase sales by lowering prices. Sometimes, as Adam Smith pointed out, you can only increase sales by reducing prices very fast. Truly a limit to the market.

I could say, this is the best strategy. I could say just do it. But you will want the reason why.

The explanation is in the more complex diagram Figure twenty-three below.

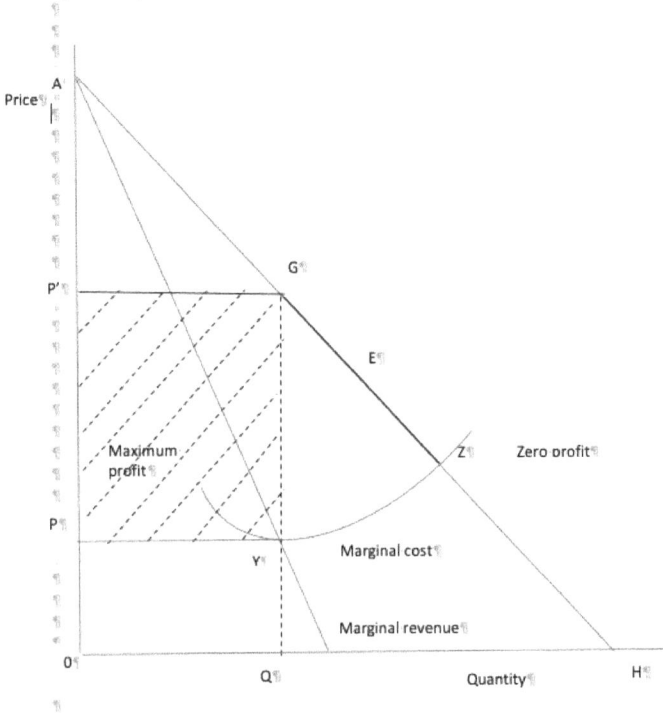

Figure twenty-three → The profit maximising flat demand curve

The firms flat demand/supply line is P'G. When it hits the sloping demand line AH, it sells down the demand line to Z, where profit is zero. In other words, the demand line hinges at G and becomes flat along P'G. In real life, when the firm's sales hit declining prices at G, it should bring in a new product and sell along the flat demand line again. This is line E.

As you can see from the above diagram there is an addition wrinkle to selling along the flat demand line. The firm should sell at the profit maximising price. Thus, for each unit quantity the firm sells, it is making the maximum profit for each unit quantity.

The profit maximising price is where the schedule of marginal costs for each unit quantity crosses the schedule of the marginal revenues for each unit quantity.

Does this profit maximising price maximise total profits for all total quantities sold in an arbitrary period compared to the alternative, selling down the sloping demand curve?

While this discussion hardly needs a diagram, it is explained in Figure twenty-four.

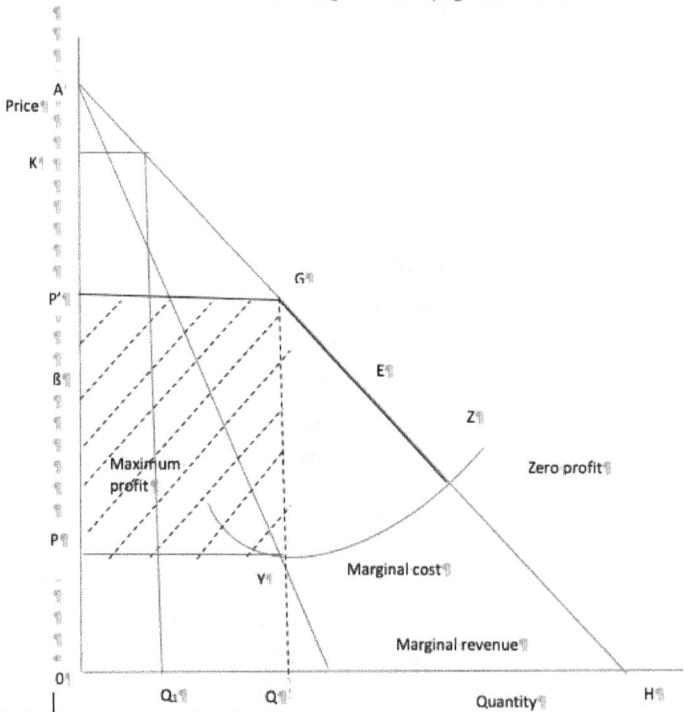

Figure twenty-four → Is selling at a profit maximising constant price more profitable than selling down the sloping demand line?

Figure 24 is the same as figure 23, except for two additions, price K above the profit maximising price G. The question is, do these prices inscribe profit quadrilaterals inscribe greater than profits sold at price G at these changed quantities. At price K quantity Q_1 is sold.

Remember the marginal cost line is the supply curve.

Now when you set marginal cost equals marginal revenue you get the profit maximising price for the *profit maximising quantity sold*. If you keep the profit maximising price constant and vary the quantity sold, say to Q_1, the market price increases to K. If you are flat pricing, the profit would be $P'NQ_1P$. You are selling below the profit maximising quantity, and the profit would be lower than the area PKQ_1P. Thus, selling along the flat price line P'G, at N, you would be making lower profits than the maximum profit.

Is it worth it?

Advantages.

1. Convenience. Since you are selling at a single price, you have no need to continuously test the market for the market price.
2. You experience excess demand to the point G, so there is no need to spend much on marketing.
3. As soon as you experience falling prices, this is the signal to introduce a new product and sell it again at constant prices. In other words, market signals guide you, and you have no need to

experience continuously falling prices with no signal where to get off.

Disadvantages

1. Lower profits than using a sloping demand line. The profits are lower by the area of the quadrilateral P'NKP.

You have to ask yourself, are greater pricing convenience, lower marketing costs and market signal to move to a new product worth more than possible higher profits?

So, what does the firm have to do if it wishes to sell at constant prices?

1. Estimate the market demand schedule for their product. (To do this you will probably to employ a competent economist for this. Competent is the word. Most economists are really not competent enough. Ask "How do you estimate a demand schedule?")
2. From the demand schedule, estimate the marginal revenue schedule.
3. From internal production data, estimate the marginal cost schedule. (You need to employ a competent account. You ask them "How do you estimate a marginal cost schedule?")
4. At the point marginal cost = marginal revenue, and estimate the profit maximising quantity.
5. From the demand schedule, use this quantity to estimate the profit maximising price.

(Your resident economist can't do this? You know what to do).

Remember, your firm has to keep doing this, so find a capable economist and a capable accountant.

CHAPTER FIFTEEN

REVENUE

From here we go to the important question of revenue, and the surprising connection with the slope of the demand line. And the lack of connection with supply.

We won't bother with another diagram. Just basic mathematics.

For the sake of argument, the firm trades with this supply/demand layout. Up to a certain quantity point the price is constant. Then after that quantity point the price declines. All this can take place in the same unit period.

In the flat price trading period, the unit price is P. Revenue is Q x P in that period when prices are flat.

Is there a maximum revenue for a flat demand line?

$$REV = Q \times P$$

$$\frac{d\,REV}{dQ} = P$$

There is no maximum revenue for a flat demand line. Revenue directly increases with increasing Q.

The formula of a straight-line downward sloping demand line with axes P and Q is

$$P = b - cQ$$

Where b is the intersection of the sloping line with the P axis, and c is the negative slope.

To obtain revenue multiply P by Q on both sides.

$$REV = P \times Q = bQ - cQ^2$$

To obtain a maximum, differentiate.

$$\frac{d\,REV}{dQ} = b - 2cQ$$

equals 0 when the quadratic curve is at its maximum.

So $b - 2cQ = 0$

The maximum is when $Q = \dfrac{b}{2c}$

Thus, revenue for a declining demand curve reaches a maximum, and then declines.

If the demand curve is a multinomial curve, the outcome is the same. The revenue maximum depends on the parameters of the demand curve.

Supply values have no influence in this outcome. The conclusion is that all firms, when they cease selling at a constant price, inevitably reach a point of maximum revenue when selling that product. A declining demand curve inevitably reaches a point of maximum revenue.

What are the implications of this result?

1. When the selling price is constant, revenue increases directly with quantity sold. There is no maximum.
2. When the firm hits a declining demand curve, you may be lucky to hit a maximum, but then a decline in revenue is a certainty. Revenue may at first increase, but then revenues <u>will</u> decline as price declines outweigh the quantity sold.
3. If you hit a region of declining revenue, <u>start selling a new or upgraded product</u>. Then you are back onto the constant price line.

It must be stressed that this result has nothing to do with profits, for which you have to bring in costs.

So, we come to an end to the theoretical section. You have learned a lot. Indeed, you now know more than most successful and rich entrepreneurs. If they have got where they are, they have succeeded by happenstance. Learning by doing. Sometimes that experience came with a bitter and costly price. You will have a model in your head to guide you.

What have you learned as the necessary thing to do?

Two things:

1. Your firm must operate under increasing returns to scale – always. You have that under your control.
2. As much as possible, sell with a flat or constant price. When you hit the wall, (the extent of the market), and have to sell at a falling price, <u>get a new product</u>.

Simple! Just two rules. All the rest, the concepts of heavy management books and Harvard MBA's, you can leave to your subordinates. These fashions change. Do this or that. Be nice to these persons or those. So, write the above two rules down, keep a copy in your secret drawer, and apply the rules always, without change. Regard the capering round of advisors, who want you to do something different, with amusement, but be rock hard on those two requirements.

PART II

ENTERPRISE AND VENTURE CAPITAL

Before we go onto a description of Enterprise and Venture Capital, there will be those who question why this book commenced and devoted over half its pages to a description of microeconomics? I could have at Chapter thirteen just jumped into a set of vague maxims, and say "just do it".

But a budding Venture Capitalist, I feel, needs a greater understanding of basic economics. Where it all fits in. More than "Just do what has worked, and everybody does this...!"

Now, hopefully, you know what Increasing Returns to Scale means, and why this is the ultimate aim of (successful) venture capital. If things go wrong, you will have some theoretical concepts in the back of your mind to guide you back to a safe haven. Don't rely on consultants with their accounting-based advice. Cutting labour costs may only work if the firm is operating under decreasing returns to scale. Calculate first if you are operating under increasing returns to scale, (using the formulae in my book "Increasing Returns to Scale" by T. Walshaw), and if you are not operating under increasing returns to scale, estimate what to do to get back to it. (You may have to reduce expenditure in capital stock).

CHAPTER SIXTEEN

ENTERPRISE

The definitions usually used for Enterprise are vague and not very useful. I shall use a definition that is more operationally useful, as follows:

Definition

"Enterprise is the action to start a firm to produce and sell a good or service, and it is intended that the firm would operate under increasing returns to scale." That is, it is intended that the firm would have employees and would operate with the division of labour.

There is no requirement for the enterprise to be original. Copy. Copy. But just do it better. There are a whole range of entrepreneurs, such as Mark Zuckerberg with Facebook and Elon Musk with electric cars, who were not original, but in some way they got to the top, and were highly successful.

A firm starting up as a sole trader, such as a truck driver, would not be under this definition be an entrepreneur, as he would not be creating wealth by the division of labour. Such a person just would be "buying a job", in the words of self-help books, and would not be able to go away for a holiday, and be able to receive an income from his business in his absence.

As has already been described, the process of wealth creation is tied up in increasing returns to scale. No increasing returns to scale, no profits, or sustainable profits over a long period. And has been seen in Chapter Eight, it is enterprise that places the firm in the zone of increasing returns to scale and thus creates wealth.

Thus Enterprise, Increasing Returns to Scale and wealth creation are ineluctably joined. Yes, you could start a small firm that does not expand as it already operates under decreasing returns to scale, and create a minimal amount of wealth. But to repeat, significant wealth is only created by increasing returns to scale, and it takes Enterprise, through action of the Entrepreneur, to do this.

Nearly all wealth creation has the prime cause of Enterprise, through the action of the Entrepreneur, creating a firm operating under increasing returns to scale. No Entrepreneur, no Enterprise, no increasing returns to scale, no wealth creation..

There are many alternative definitions of wealth, such as money, resources, land, population, education and human capital, cumulated stock of research, and many other valuable stocks. But stocks depreciate in value. Every year, unless wealth creation is maintained, the value of these stocks of "wealth" can decline.

Demand in the economy is only maintained or increased by the creation of new wealth. Wealth in society is maintained and increased solely by entrepreneurial activity.

It is thus necessary to maintain a minimum level of entrepreneurial activity. If this is not done, insufficient new wealth is created. Overall demand falls. Prices falls. The value of wealth stocks decline. All value in the economy is maintained by the flow of wealth creation, which is ultimately dependent on the amount of Enterprise in the economy, which ultimately dependent on the number and activities of the Entrepreneurs in the economy. The more entrepreneurs, the more wealth.

So, what is an Entrepreneur, and what does he do? For that we go to the following chapter.

CHAPTER SEVENTEEN

THE ENTREPRENEUR

Over the years the definitions of the entrepreneur tended to be vague, limited and often contradictory. An improved definition is necessary.

In the previous chapter we described Enterprise. How is the definition of the Entrepreneur connected to this definition?   And is not sufficient to say that an Entrepreneur is "enterprising"!

Definition

"An Entrepreneur is a person who takes action to start a firm to produce and sell goods or services that will operate under increasing returns to scale".

It was often assumed from definitions used elsewhere that this Entrepreneur must bring together the necessary resources, and also provide the necessary planning and management; but as can be seen in the next chapters on Venture Capital, these requirements are not necessary all. Many recent Venture Capital inceptions required zero capital input by the entrepreneur, and in many cases their management input was rapidly excluded.

For many years the entrepreneur was defined as a "capitalist", providing the necessary capital and management control. This definition is entirely inaccurate. Entrepreneurs can and often do provide neither capital nor management.

It is noted that an integral component of the above definition is increasing returns to scale. Without increasing returns to scale, the entrepreneur's firm would not create wealth for himself and society. It would rapidly cease to exist. The entrepreneur would become a non-entrepreneur!

What about Venture Capitalists? They have a hand in starting numerous enterprises. Are they "multi-entrepreneurs"? No. A venture capitalist is an entrepreneur when he starts his venture capital firm, but after that all these start-ups are the product of these venture capital firms. They churn ventures out like bolts of cloth (the modern venture capital firm such as Y-Combinator really does this). It is an industry, on which the venture capital firms make profits starting many new ventures.

Now that we have defined an Entrepreneur, what are the entrepreneur's required characteristics? How can they be described?

For this purpose, we need a list of the characteristics of an entrepreneur in the order of importance, or at least the requirements in order needed to start the enterprise. It is of course assumed that the putative entrepreneur should be healthy and active, but not necessarily young. But Ray Croc started McDonalds at the age of 52!

Table 2   In my opinion, the characteristics of an entrepreneur in order of inception of the enterprise are:

These characteristics are all probably equally important at one time or another. They are in the order of timing in the growth of the firm.

1. Courage
2. Desires money
3. Desires independence
4. Motivated and persistent
5. Opportunist
6. Finder and user of innovations
7. Initiator
8. Possibly supplies a small amount of capital, but in the modern venture capital environment, this is no longer necessary
9. Personal honesty
10. Organiser and builder
11. Leader
12. Reacts immediately to change

These characteristics are described as follows.

1. Courage. For an entrepreneur to be a risk-taker he needs personal courage. The entrepreneur needs to take a risk with his lifestyle. This is the original and most usual definition. The entrepreneur needs to risk money, time and

other interests with the aim of gaining money and personal satisfaction.

However, many people take risks all the time. Some gamble, others take risks with their careers, some take physical risks for monetary gain or sheer enjoyment. These are not entrepreneurs.

2. Desires money. Psychological surveys say that the desire for more money is an overwhelming motivator for entrepreneurs. Initially they desire financial security for themselves and their family, and then greater status. However, surveys of successful entrepreneurs show that past a certain point, the desire for more money does not concern them.

3. Desires independence. To be your own boss. Psychological surveys of entrepreneurs show that the desire for independence is an overwhelming desire, after the desire for money, that motivates an entrepreneur to go out on their own. While everybody desires more money, most are happy to continue to take orders. Their desire for independence is not so overwhelming that they are willing to take the risk and upset their lives to go out on their own. An additional issue is that the vast majority of beings are social animals, and are unwilling to lose their social connections to, at least initially, work on their own. An entrepreneur is much less socially inclined, and has a far greater desire to be their own boss.

4. Motivated, active and persistent. This is a pre-requisite. An entrepreneur needs to be a person who constantly takes action, and does not let things slide. If they let extraneous events take priority, and if the can be pushed around, they will get nowhere. As all self-help books say, persistence is the pre-requisite for success.

5. Opportunist. An entrepreneur, at least initially, must seek new opportunities and take advantage of them. A successful continuing entrepreneur must continue to be an opportunist. Not many have this mindset – constantly looking for new opportunities. An entrepreneur must be an opportunist – and act quickly with courage.

6. Finder and user of innovations. An entrepreneur must be an innovator. The best opportunities for an entrepreneur are in the vast un-tapped universe of novel goods and services, where there is no initial competition so there are monopoly rents and large profits. True, a successful entrepreneur can still operate in known areas, such as selling franchises, or for example setting up a department store. Many just copy. But the most successful entrepreneurs are visionaries, innovators and opportunists.

7. Initiator. Not a follower. This is a sub-category of courage. If something is perceived to be needed to be done, the entrepreneur is the first to say

that it needs to be done and what is to be done, and if necessary does it himself.

8. Supplier of capital – maybe. From the days of Adam Smith it was assumed that an entrepreneur must be a capitalist. Being an entrepreneur and a capitalist was considered synonymous. Not anymore. Nowadays, with the growth of venture capital, the needed financial contribution of entrepreneurs has fallen from very little in the days of Allen Noyce and Steve Jobs in the 1970's to nothing at all. It is rare for venture capitalists nowadays to ask for a financial contribution from the putative entrepreneur. Money is cheap, and investors are desperate to throw their money at anything potentially profitable. Capital is no longer part of the entrepreneurial makeup.

9. Personal honesty. We are now getting down to a basic characteristic of a successful entrepreneur. This should be at the very start, but regrettably a lot of personally dishonest entrepreneurs can create successful start-ups. But after that things go wrong. It is noteworthy that ALL successful Venture Capitalists look for personal honesty as the PRIME requisite for any entrepreneur they invest in, far above "bankable" ideas. This is from bitter experience. As one said "We are not paying for excuses, laziness, dishonesty, character defects. They can prove very costly." Most venture capitalists check the CV very carefully.

10. Organiser and builder. At the start the organisation has to be built from scratch. At the start the entrepreneur has to be the sole manager. He has to build a firm that employs people, then divides the roles, which then makes the product and sells it. Not many people, when they have come this far, can change from being a thinker to a doer, and being an organiser.

11. Leader. And yes, that entrepreneur must be a leader. Especially eventually if he has many managers beneath him. He must change again to someone who inspires subordinates to agree with the goals set by the entrepreneur, and actively work towards them.

12. Reacts immediately to change. Change happens. The entrepreneur must rapidly react to change. This is easier said than done. An entrepreneur can get comfortable with his achievements, and become oblivious to the need for change. The entrepreneur has a need to set up an efficient communications system, a system that communicates the need for change not only from outside the firm, but also from inside. There must be fast and efficient communication of the need for change from the bottom up. All organizations must change, and change rapidly and be responsive when there is a need for change – or the firm will expire.

On this latter requirement, an outstandingly successful entrepreneur told me the reason why his firm is continuously successful, and is at the forefront of growth and change. He set up locked "suggestion boxes" throughout his firm, emptied regularly by people from his personal office, "The Secretariat". He called these boxes cynically his "Triccotteur Boxes". They have a dual purpose. Not only supplying new ideas (for substantial rewards), but reports of bad behaviour and corruption in the firm. For years now, he said, he has had minimal issues of personal abuse or fraud.

This list describes the basic requirements of a successful entrepreneur. Many desire to be a successful entrepreneur. Few succeed.

CHAPTER EIGHTEEN

THE HISTORY OF THE USE OF THE NAME ENTREPRENEUR

The concept of the entrepreneur has been greatly neglected in economics. Yes, the entrepreneur is occasionally mentioned, but then is sidelined. He is an "economic actor" that automatically does this task of organising, risk taking and providing capital, but his role is taken for granted. There are no real consequences for his role. Does the entrepreneur create wealth? Not under constant returns to scale. Under these conditions his role would be exploitive. It would only be the workers that create value, as again, there would be no increasing returns to scale.

This is not to say workers do not create wealth. But not all of them create wealth. Workers in organisations operating under increasing returns to scale create wealth. Workers in organisations operating under decreasing returns to scale create wealth as long as that organisation is profitable. All the rest of workers, operating under unprofitable decreasing returns to scale and declining returns to scale, consume wealth. They are among that part of society who are consuming and not producing.

If you ask, "What proportion of the wealth created by these workers goes back to them?", in this enquiry we will sidestep the question of distribution (exploitation?).

This massive subject in economics has not been resolved. What is a "fair" distribution of the wealth created between the workers and the legal owners of the productive organisation? How is it to be done? Is the proposed re-distribution/wage raising economically efficient? Or to put it another way, which aim is better, the one that maximises the welfare of workers the most? Faster growth or greater re-distribution? Whoever provides a believable solution to this major question will certainly gain a Nobel Prize.

All I would say is that is proportion is set by the market at the time, in proportion to demand and supply for the various resources, including various types of labor.

Indeed, does it matter, if both sides are gaining?

I might add, many successful entrepreneurs issue shares to all their employees, in proportion to the amount of pay in the previous year and the length of service. How much? This can be substantial. Furthermore, often these shares and dividends are locked into their retirement funds, and can only be accessed for certain things – buying a home or their children's education. Getting a car? Nope. Many of these long-term employees have retired millionaires, but most elect to keep balance of the money in the "fund" after buying an annuity.

This is not charity. One entrepreneur I know says these share distributions increase work and motivation, as well as that very important but neglected factor, loyalty. He says that they have increased his firm's profit by at least 30 per cent.

A short history of the use of the term "Entrepreneur"

Discussion of the role and definition of the entrepreneur goes back a long way. The history of the subject has been subject to various cycles of interest and neglect, until in the past thirty years there has been a resurgence of interest. However, this resurgence originated from areas of psychology and business management, not economics. Economic scholarship cannot get a hang of this subject, it seems, and it is still preoccupied with the concepts of equilibrium and pure competition.

Richard Cantillon (in 1725), an early very brilliant monetary economist, who made a fortune selling out shares in John Law's Mississippi scheme. He was the inventor of the term 'entrepreneur', French for undertaker. He defined this person as an agent who takes the risk buys products to combine them into other products. He linked risk, time, organisational ability, and the supplier of capital. His essay "Essai sur la Nature de Commerce en Général" (Cantillon 1725) referred to the "entrepreneur" as a person who bought cheaply at a certain price and sold output at an uncertain price.

Adam Smith (1776) defined an entrepreneur "is a proprietary capitalist, a supplier of capital and at the same time, works as a manager intervening between labour and capital". However, Smith in his foundational Chapter One on the pin factory assumes the factory's existence, and does not discuss the role of the factory's owner and manager. This was the start of a long record of economic thought – assume something was already in place.

Jean Baptiste Say (1803) (of Say's Law "increased supply creates increased demand") goes into further detail. "An entrepreneur is the economic agent who unites all means of production, the land of one, the labour of another and the capital of yet another and thus produces a product. By selling the product in the market, he pays rent of land, wages of labor, interest on capital and what remiss is his profit". Whew! Say thus emphasized the functions of the entrepreneur as co-ordination, organisation and supervision.

Then nothing happens in economics for nearly ninety years. While Jeremy Bentham and John Stuart Mill mentioned the entrepreneur in passing, the concept was not central to their attempts at price theory. Economics went down a rabbit hole of the theory of value and distribution, and didn't come up for air until Marshall (1890) crossed supply and demand to obtain price. Yes, economists also discussed utility theory and the elasticity of supply and demand, and got all mathematical with General Equilibrium. But production theory was at a dead end, held back by the concept of Constant returns to scale. But Marshall again briefly reintroduced the concept of entrepreneurship as an organiser and coordinator.

The concept of entrepreneur stagnated until in 1921 Frank Knight in his book "Risk, Uncertainty and Profit" argued that the skills of the entrepreneur lay in the in his ability to handle uncertainty. Risk of course was measurable and could be priced.

Again, things died the death until Joseph Schumpeter (1934) assigned for the first time a crucial role of innovator to the entrepreneur in his book "Theory of Economic Development". According to Schumpeter, entrepreneurship is essentially a creative activity. The entrepreneur is the innovator who introduces something new into the economy. He tried to develop an entirely new economic theory based on change, as opposed to equilibrium. He discussed the function of an entrepreneur as an individual who tends to break the equilibrium by introducing innovations into the system. He argued that "creative destruction is the essential fact of capitalism" and the entrepreneur is the prime agent of economic change.

Hayek (1945) and von Mises (1949) tried to raise the question of entrepreneurship, but nobody listened.

Frederick Harbison in his paper "Entrepreneurial Organisation as a Factor" (1951) placed the entrepreneur at the centre as an organisation builder and leader.

Arthur Cole, an economics professor at Harvard, tried to raise the study of entrepreneurial history through "Journal of Economic History" and his founding of the Harvard Research Center on Economic History, but both died in 1958.

David McClelland, a psychologist, was the first green shoot in the study of entrepreneurial questions in his book "The Achieving Society" (1961). This generated a stream of publications on the subject on the "traits" of individual entrepreneurs.

Baumol (1968) was one of the first economists who tried to re-integrate the entrepreneurial function into economics. He said "There is no room in standard economics for enterprise or initiative. The management group becomes a passive calculation that reacts mechanically to external developments over which it does not exert, and does not even attempt to exert any influence" (p. 67). "The theoretical firm is entrepreneurless – The Prince of Denmark has been expunged from the discussion of Hamlet" (p. 66). The neo-classical model is essentially an instrument of optimality analysis, "maximisation and minimisation have consolidated the foundation of the theory, (but) as a result of this fact the theory is deprived of the ability to possess an analysis of entrepreneurship (p 68).

It was not until Schumpetarian analysis made a comeback in the 1970's in the form of evolutionary economics that the entrepreneur began to make a headway in being incorporated in economic design (Klein 1977) (Nelson and Winter 1982).

From the early 1980's there began an explosion of literature on the subject of entrepreneurs that was connected to the study of small start-ups. However, the study of entrepreneurship remained highly fragmented, with a minimal relationship with economics. The major influences were studies in business management, psychology, social anthropology and finance.

In the past three decades there have been many papers and books written on the subject. Outstanding ones include W. Casson, 1982 "The Entrepreneur: An Economic Theory", PH Brockhaus 1982 "The psychology of an entrepreneur", DC Blanchfloss and AT Oswald, 1988, "What makes an Entrepreneur", DL Sexton and P Kassandra, (Eds), 1992 "The state of the art of entrepreneurships", DC Blanchflower and AJ Oswald 1998, Journal of Labor Economics "What makes an entrepreneur", SJ Parker 2018 "The economics of entrepreneurship". The subject has exploded in recent years, and there are currently at least half a dozen university courses in entrepreneurship.

But the connection with economics remains small. A survey of the literature by Carlson et al (2013) found that economics related papers on entrepreneurship made up of only about two percent of the total. There remained a strong inhibition in the economics profession preventing economists taking an interest in the subject of entrepreneurship.

CHAPTER NINETEEN

VENTURE CAPITAL INVESTING

What is Venture Capital investing? Again, we need a definition.

Definition

"Venture Capital investing is the activity of financing new potentially profitable ventures proposed by persons with proposals for these ventures".

As can be seen from the above definition, Venture Capital is an investment process, most usually done by a firm, not an individual, that invests in new ventures as a continuing business. The venture capital firm receives business proposals from persons outside the firm, assesses them, and decides whether or not to invest in these proposals. If the venture capital firm does decide to invest, it goes through a standard procedure of deciding how much to invest, and the form of this investment including deciding on the structure of the investment and whether or not the venture capital firm would provide management supervision.

The essential core of successful venture capital investing is:

1. Discover which potential investments have a flat(ish) demand curve.
2. Whether the firm will operate under increasing returns to scale.

That's all.

Many hundreds of books have been written about successful venture capital investing. They go on and on about discerning risk, and ascertaining how much capital you require, discerning the capabilities and characters of your potential partners, how to motivate your employees. Yes, they can be important. But only if the enterprise is marginal. If the startup enterprise is highly profitable, a lot can and does be forgiven, at least for a while.

In recent times, a plethora of new venture capital firms have started up. That is good. However, no consistent or successful criterion for a successful venture investment has been decided upon. From what I have seen the general concept is a "bankable idea", plus some close connection with technology and computers. Unfortunately, using these criteria, 80 per cent of startups are unsuccessful. Those that do succeed, succeed for no apparent reason. "The time was right". "They were first". Vague nostrums like that.

For the venture capital industry to succeed, and consistently invest in successful ventures, it must find a workable and profitable rationale. Yes, new technology opens up a vast new continent of unexploited demand. Or it has in the past. But my perception is that the supply of technological innovations is rapidly exceeding the demand for them. New unexploited areas of unrequited demand need to be found.

Whatever new area is found, cosmetics, cars, food, it must have the above two simple criteria. A long flat(ish) demand curve, and the good may be supplied under increasing returns to scale. Only then will success be almost certainly guaranteed.

If the enterprise fits the first two criteria above it *will* rapidly take off

and:
1. If the enterprise is immediately successful, there is NO risk involved. (Less than going to work as an employee – as one entrepreneur told me, if thing go wrong, I will be the last to be fired.)
2. You won't require much capital, as Robert Kiyosaki says, (Kiyosaki (1992)), or in many circumstances, none at all. Forget the employee mindset "I need money". You will find that banks and money lenders will throw money at you from an early stage. You will after you have got going, like Steve Jobs, find it difficult to refuse investment offers.
3. The characters and capabilities of your partners. That is actually a killer. Very few people (less than 20%), from my experience, are naturally hardworking and honest when they lack an external incentive to perform. What keeps the rest on track is the necessity to earn a pay packet, and not be fired. Don't believe verbal promises. "A verbal promise is not worth the paper it written on".

Instead of going down the psychology route, I have found the best method is to put everyone on employee mode. Put their promised goals on paper, together with penalties. Give them a copy. (They will laugh "ha,ha,ha" the first couple of times, then there will be clear resentment), but you say that "if you do not perform, our partnership will be terminated, as per our partnership agreement, blah, blah, blah". Tough, but it is better than crying later.

However, it is best not to have partners. See the above paragraph about capital. Have a number of trusted paid employees. "A brains trust", as advocated by Andrew Carnegie. But they work for a salary. They are used to it. It is also a very good idea to motivate staff by offering them shares in some form. You will be amazed how much this changes their attitude and performance.

4. Employee motivation. Hundreds of books have been written on this. But they are all United States centred. What if your factory is in China or Japan? Totally different. Even moving the production to Mexico leads to personnel problems. My advice is to find a local competent and experienced manager, and have local people in ALL management and supervisory roles. Indeed, if you have plants located in different parts of the United States, it is best to have all managers born and bred in that locality.

We have discussed the flat demand line and the limit of the market with Figure 22. I must reinforce this advice. It applies to YOU. No ifs and buts. Whether your firm supplies software or is a department store, ALL firms follow the same path. A period when there appears to be unlimited demand for your product, you are in the land of milk and honey. But then demand begins to fall. Yes, you can continue selling by reducing prices. And if you have no alternative product, you must get one. Get a new product. Fast.

In fact, you should always have a new product ready in the wings. That is what R&D is all about. Most surviving firms have learnt that lesson from bitter experience. You are not in the business of scientific improvement. You are in the business of survival. Your R&D division is your insurance division. Without R&D, your firm will die.

What you do is what most companies have learned to do from bitter experience. Henry Ford learned this lesson when he refused to stop making the Model T in the late 1920's. His sales and revenues declined, no matter how fast he reduced the price of the Model T.

You need a new improved model, a Gen 6, so that you go back to selling on the flat demand curve. It has been a rule of the thumb that for a venture capitalist investing in software that a flat demand curve is almost a certainty. You need only look at the repeated generations of Microsoft software. Even Bill Gates needs to update his software regularly.

However, the problem in recent times is that there is absolutely no demand for certain types of software – at any price. So, you have to test the market. But the risks are small. If the software does not initially sell, the loss is generally small.

Another source of a flat demand curve is exporting, as you extend the "extent of the market". If you have a free trade area, exporting in physical goods in containers is relatively cheap. That is why Chinese manufacturing has succeeded so well. Not because of cheap labour.

In summary there are two diagrams a potential venture capitalist needs to keep in mind. There are two. Just two. It is pretty simple. Figure 25 (a) and (b).

Figure twenty-five   →   The Two Diagrams that should be kept in mind when investing in New Enterprises

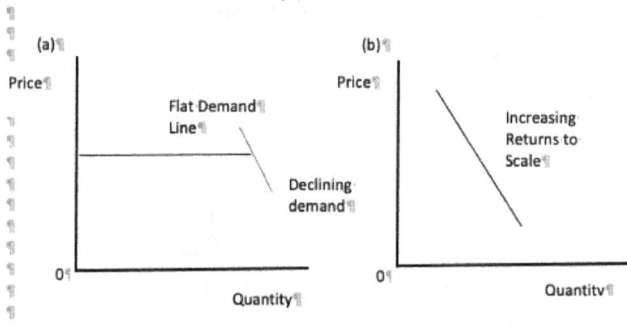

The first, and most important, is the slope of the potential demand curve. Is it flat? Figure (a).

The second is Figure (b), the returns to scale curve. you get increasing returns to scale, as you employ more people and you get increasing division of labour. The tasks are divided into small and smaller portions for each employee, and thus increase productivity. How long can this continue? This is a management problem. Sooner or later management gets slack and complaisant, and returns to scale stops and decreasing returns to scale starts. There is no intermediation of constant returns to scale.

This is not just a theoretical problem. After Steve Job's death, Apple, for example, back in 2013, went on an employment spending spree. The number of employees shot up. As a consequence, Apple entered decreasing returns to scale and a region of falling profits. As a consequence, Apple struggled for the next few years. To compound that, Apple hit a declining demand and falling prices for its major product, its cell or mobile phones. A double whammy!

The above two diagrams are what the venture capitalist, or potential venture capitalists, should always keep in mind. All other issues, costs, debt (you really shouldn't have much), management, personnel issues, are really side issues compared to the above – demand for your product, and are you continuing to operate in increasing returns?

You must make absolutely sure that you can operate in and remain in increasing returns to scale. If you re-engineer the formulae in Chapter 12, you can make sure of that.

But you must retain complete control over all your internal production activities. Outsourcing it to some firm such as Foxconn is a recipe for disaster. It is as if you have a whole production division over which you do not control the inputs. What is worse, you do not gain the benefits of increasing returns to scale. Your contractor will offer you a fixed price contract. Whatever the consultants say, this behaviour is not in the least bit clever. They are your inputs. You must control them.

Yes, there is a limit to your market. It will become evident when you can only sell your product at lower prices. That is a worry. You need a new product.

Another piece of useful advice. The 80/20 rule. After your firm has grown past the eponymous 150 employee mark, you will find that 20 per cent of your products bring in 80 per cent of your profits, and indeed, 20 per cent of your employees, (usually the ones at the bottom), produce 80 percent of your profits. Your major job, as the guy at the top of a firm who may be running out of puff, is to identify both the best products and the best employees, and then go away, and decide what to do about it.

So, in summary, success in venture capitalism is almost solely due to two factors
- Whether the potential demand curve for your product has a flat or near flat demand curve
- Whether you can maintain production or output in the firm under increasing returns to scale.

Simple. But how many venture capital projects fail because they have not met one or more of these criteria? Certainly, all the failures. Bad management, high costs, or changing marketing conditions are just excuses.

CHAPTER TWENTY

THE VENTURE CAPITAL PROCESS

This chapter goes into more detail of the venture capital process. It has now become pretty standardised, as it has become an industry. Venture proposals in one end, startups out the other. And it is a highly profitable industry.

At this point any stories of the history and the current functioning of the venture capital market goes into jargon. The jargon and methodology have become standardised, but to a non-venture capitalist these terms are still a mystery. So, I have decided to start with the framework of venture capitalism, and a description how it works.

Table 3   The Venture Capital Process

The idea	It all starts here. The entrepreneur has an idea. Then the entrepreneur approaches an angel investor with his/her idea for financing. The entrepreneurs need not supply any financing for the enterprise.
Angel investing	Angel investors supply a relatively small amount of

money. But nowadays this amount has increased in value up to $100,000. The angel investor helps set up the company, and provides some element of advice and help.

Series A — After the enterprise has begun production and sales, this Series is the first set of investments from initial investors. The shares of the enterprise have increased in value, and the Series A investors pay an increased price per share.

Series B — The worth of the company has greatly expanded, and the Series B investors pay a much higher price per share. Total investment could be around $100 million.

IPO — Public float. The public is invited to invest in an issue of shares in the company that will be traded on the stock exchange. From now on the company will be valued at this quoted share price.

The above is the basic investment structure that has evolved in the Venture Capital headquarters in Silicon

Valley. There could be more Series of investment, Series C and so on, but this is unusual. There is a strong desire from investors to have an IPO (Initial Public Offer) quickly, so that they can cash out. Though many wait longer in the hope of obtaining an increased share price.

So, what is the description of the process?

"In the beginning was the idea, and the idea was with the entrepreneur".

The first step is that an entrepreneur has a potentially profitable idea. At this stage the idea may be just in his head, and not even on paper. There is not necessarily even a company, or even a business plan. (What's that?).

The next stage is that the entrepreneur wants to start production and sales, and for that he needs capital. He has to approach other potential investors. These initial investors are called Angel Investors.

Until very recently, Angel investors were few and fearful. But the market has evolved and massively changed. The supply of Angel investors has greatly increased, largely because of the initial influence of Paul Graham and his Angel investing firm Y-Combinator. (More of this later). Now that investors have seen how potentially profitable Angel investing can be, there are a large number of copyists. As a result, nowadays, your entrepreneur in most locations has little difficulty raising initial investments for a high proportion of proposals. This development has been highly beneficial for society and the economy as a whole.

While the initial investments of Angel investments are usually relatively small (though this amount has grown to be up to $100,000), the potential relative gains are high as the enterprise moves into Series A investment or Series B investment.

However, it must be stressed that a high proportion of Angel investments do not succeed at this point. Y-Combinator has published a useful list of reasons for enterprise failure. These are:

Table 4   Reasons for enterprise failure

1. There is no market need for the idea
        42%
2. The enterprise runs out of cash
        29%
3. The enterprise does not have the right team
        23%
4. The enterprise gets outcompeted
        19%
5. Pricing/cost issues
        18%
6. Poor quality product
        17%
7. The enterprise lacks a business model/plan
        17%
8. Poor marketing
        14%
9. The entrepreneurs ignore customer suggestions
        14%

10. The product mis-timed/too early
    13%
11. The management lose focus/get tired
    13%
12. Pivot gone bad
    10%
13. The entrepreneurs lack/lose passion
    9%
14. Bad Location
    9%
15. There is disharmony among team/investors
    8%
16. No Financing due to lack of Investor Interest
    8%
17. Legal Challenges
    8%
18. The entrepreneurs don't use Network/Advisors
    8%
19. Management burn out
    8%
20. Failure to Pivot
    7%

There can be two or more simultaneous reasons for failure.

Except for the first two reasons, no market and running out of cash, most of the reasons for failure are personal, not financial, as was previously commonly supposed. Character problems and bad judgement. And even running out of cash is really caused by bad management and bad judgement.

No market for the idea? As long as you can sell above marginal cost (you know what that is) you can still survive and grow. Many firms I have seen go bust are incapable of pricing. (You can do that now, can't you?) It's not just a guess. (Huh, what's marginal cost?)

As Peter Thiel, the VC investor, (discussed later) decided, it is not worth his time, effort and resources to sort out the personal issues of the enterprise founders. He discovered that the best policy for his VC firm was to fund a large number of startups, and let the failures die without putting in much effort to keep them alive.

A question many people ask is "What proportion of the initial startup's shares does the Angel investor get"? The answer is that this proportion has massively fallen from around 80% or more in the 1950's to about 6% with Y-Combinator. The trade-off is that while the VC of old would hunt around for highly paid CEO's to the manage the firm, and put up with the original company founders not washing, having board meetings in hot tubs and coming to meetings in pyjamas, nowadays this behaviour is not tolerated. These same founders are left to sink or swim. The VC calculation is that even if 90 out of 100 startups fail because of the behavioural failures of the company founders, they will still make a big profit.

The next step is Series A. Those firms that survive to this stage are hawked around among the Angel investor's list of wealthy individuals and interested organisations, and are asked if they are willing to invest in shares in this company. These individuals and organisations need to be legally capable to invest in these high-risk investments. This is a legal issue that varies from country to country, and I won't go into it. These investments are high risk because even at this stage the company could fail. However, these shares would even at this stage be worth a lot more than the Angel investor paid for them.

A related issue is whether these shares are a new issue, or taken from the existing stock of shares held by the Angel investor and the founders. From the economic point of view it makes no difference, but it is amazing how much the original shareholders and lawyers are hung up about this issue.

The firm continues to do well, and there is usually a second round of Share issues – Series B. Again, at a higher price. The buyers of these shares need not be the same sort of buyers as those for the Series A. But it is the same process. These early issues are high risk, but they can be very profitable.

This process can continue for Series C, Series D, and so on, but by this time the original shareholders would be getting toey and demanding an IPO.

The IPO, the Initial Public Offer, is something different. The shares are offered to the general public in a float, to be usually listed on a Stock Exchange. An issue of new shares is usually made, and they are offered to the general public at either a fixed price, or more unusually, at some form of auction. The treatment varies though there is a general standard. The price of these shares exceeds the share prices paid by the original investors. It is often made certain that the founders and original investors have free bonus share allocated to them. There are also "vested" shares and share options for the founders and many employees. There is not set formula. Except that the outcome is usually highly profitable for the company founders and original investors.

Recently there has been an interesting development in the VC industry. The VCs are turning into large investment banks. The most successful Venture Capitalist companies, such as Peter Theil's Founders Funds or Paul Graham's Y-Combinator are now worth many billions of Dollars. The Wall Street Journal said on December 29 2022 that the venture capital industry had a stockpile of $539 billion cash. Due to their success, venture capital companies are rapidly transforming into large and very powerful investment banks. While normal investment banks make a good living trading in the financial markets, the venture capital participants are using investments in entrepreneurial companies to make money at a more rapid rate. Nevertheless, they will have to find a profitable short-term use for all this cash. As such they will begin to compete with the normal investment banks. VC companies have access to vast quantities of newly created wealth, while the best the normal investment banks can do is borrow funds or rely of many years of accumulated capital. If the venture capital companies are competently managed, they are likely to outcompete the previous model of investment banks. They already exceed their value.

CHAPTER TWENTY-ONE

THE HISTORY OF VENTURE CAPITAL

It is necessary to know how the Venture Capital industry evolved to understand how it operates. And evolved it did. The industry itself could have taken-off in several directions, and may have had many different types of investors. But evolution constrained it to one location at the start and one structure. And no, it was not a corporation. But once it opted on this successful format, the system was highly successful.

The Venture Capital industry did not start in Silicon Valley, nor did it start with the present structure. It started far away in Boston, in 1944, and its father was George Doriot, who established American Research and Development (ARD), a publicly listed venture vehicle. Doriot was a Harvard Business School professor. For each new enterprise, ARD would provide a $70,000 equity investment and a $30,000 loan in return for 70% of the company. ARD made a few successful investments such as Amgen and Digital Equipment Corporation, and the company multiplied the value of its original investment by 30 times. Nevertheless, ARD was a public company, and at the time this type of investment was not highly regarded by the investing public. As a result, its quoted share value was less than its accumulated liquidation value, so as a result, in 1972, ARD was liquidated. So, this type of VC company died.

On the West Coast, back in 1957, a revolt was brewing. The founder of Shockley Semiconductor Laboratory, William Shockley, was a despot. To cut the story short, after much misgiving, eight senior researchers left to start a new company, Fairchild Semiconductor. The midwife was Arthur Rock, of what became the first genuine venture capital company, Heydon Stone. For this purpose, it raised money from Shane Fairchild, of Fairchild Cameras and Instruments. The "traitorous eight" were each asked to raise $500 for 500 $1 shares, (a big sum in those days) and Fairchild raised $1.4 million, and obtained options to pay $3 million for the traitorous eight's shares. Three years later Fairchild exercised that option, paying each of the eight $600,000.

Arthur Rock's firm transformed into Davis and Rock, a limited partnership for taxation reasons, that also had a limited life. These partners included 6 of the 8 traitorous Fairchild engineers. Without going into too many details, they founded Intel, Data Systems and Teledyne among many other successful firms. Arthur Rock did very well, and was known to have a butler at his house above Palo Alto! Davis and Rock moved the VC industry to Sandhills Road in Silicon Valley. Another innovation was that Rock insisted that all initial employees be given shares or options in the startup. Later on, VC's started vesting these shares – that is delaying the allocation of tranches of these shares. However, this led to problems. A third innovation that Rock introduced was to impose an outside CEO on the startup. While this may appear necessary, it was an extra expense, and long VC experience showed that the imposition of outside CEO's on the founders had varied success.

The firm Davis and Rock was terminated in 1968. Both Davis and Rock retired, though Rock continued to have considerable influence in the VC industry.

The first permanent partnership was Kleiner Perkins, founded by Tom Perkins and Eugene Kleiner in 1972. Perkins was the general manager of Hewlett Packard's computer division while Kleiner was one of the traitorous eight previously discussed. Perkins tracked down Kleiner and persuaded him to partner him in a VC enterprise. They raised $8.4 million and after a few unsuccessful startups, they started Tandem Computers, a systems software company, and then Genentech, a gene technology firm to produce artificial insulin. Both these companies were highly successful. With Genentech a new VC technique evolved. This was to deal with what Perkins called "dealing with white hot risks" at a staged rate. The biggest technological and scientific risks were identified stage by stage, and instead of giving the startup a large sum at the start, limited funding was also provided stage by stage. In the case of Genentech, most of the research was outsourced by contract, as the firm itself owned limited facilities.

By this time a number of copycat Venture Capitalists had started. The most outstanding at this date was Sequoia Capital, founded by Don Valentine in 1974. He started his career at Fairchild Semiconductor, moved to the startup National Semiconductor, was recruited by an investment fund Capital Research and Management, and then in 1974 decided to start his own VC, Sequoia Capital. He raised $5 million from various sources, including Rockefeller University, then cast around for a suitable startup. He found Atari, manufacturer of the primitive computer game Pong. The eccentric owners had discouraged other potential VC investors, but Valentine persevered. Sequoia invented the first Series A investment, and then sold Atari to Warner Brothers for a good profit. The next of Sequoia's successes was Cisco, another firm with strange entrepreneurs that they fostered. The founders of Cisco, Leonard Bosack and Sandy Lerner, were highly eccentric. Bosack was autistic while Lerner had a habit of calling employees "brain dead". Nevertheless, Cisco's product, a software system that coordinated different software and made them talk to each other, was in massive demand. In the end, there was another employee revolt. Valentine was told by all the Cisco engineers, "Either Lerner goes, or we go". Lerner went. Unfortunately, as she had not lasted her full contracted employment term, she lost one third of her vested shares.

By this time, the early 90's, the VC structure was pretty well established. Angel investing, Series A, Series B, IPO. There were a few highly profitable investments, a larger number of moderately successful investments, and a tail of unprofitable ventures. The success record followed a "power law" as below.

Figure twenty-six →   →   The Power Curve of Venture Capital Revenues

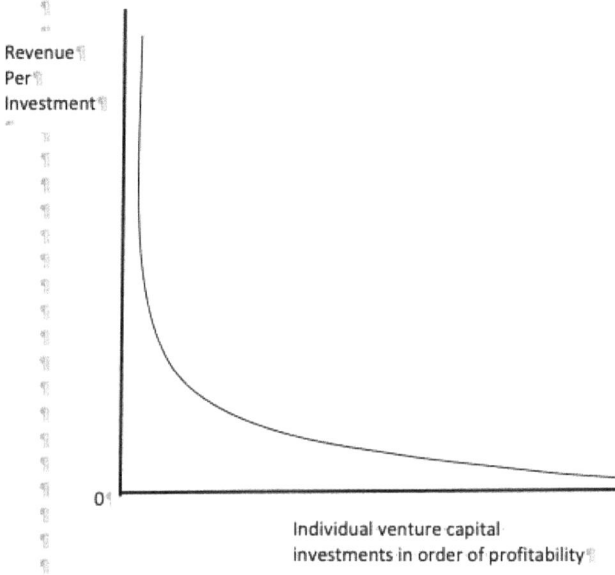

Revenue
Per
Investment

0

Individual venture capital
investments in order of profitability

In the VC business, the bonanzas (in VC parlance "the unicorns") are few. There are a far greater number of moderate successes, and a very large number of unprofitable failures.

As an aside (another aside!), many venture investors go by the 80/20 rule, as advocated by Richard Koch who wrote a book on this subject. He claimed his financial fortune grew using this rule. Only 20% of venture investments are worthwhile. A useful rule of the thumb, maybe, but the power law is a lot more informative. But you do need precise data if you are involved in large scale investment. Y-Combinator has it, but they are not giving it out.

The VC company has to set the gains against the losses. However, by carefully controlling the losses, even quickly closing down enterprises that were failing, the average venture capital company at the time made an average gain of 20% per annum. And there was a chance of making a major gain. All that was required was to follow the established system. The VC industry was mature and highly profitable.

But the VC industry changed again. It evolved into a system of large-scale support for start-up entrepreneurs. It was not realised at the time, but entrepreneurs themselves were a vast source of wealth, unicorns or not. The source of wealth was entrepreneurialism. The first to supply this large-scale support (by near accident) was Peter Thiel in the late 1990's. By 2022 he was reputed to be the richest man in the United States. Another, Paul Graham, set up what was intended to be a near charity to support startups, Y-Combinator, in 2005, and by 2022 Y-Combinator was worth $14 billion. This pair had hit on the philosopher's stone! Supporting large numbers of entrepreneurs with few restrictions was a vast source of wealth. The more entrepreneurs, the more money they made. The old days of careful selection and supervision were gone.

Peter Thiel had two degrees from Stanford, drifted in and out of derivatives trading in New York, drifted back to the West Coast, started a small hedge fund, and contributed to the libertarian Stanford Review. After giving a lecture on currency trading at Stanford, he met Steve Levchin who pitched him the idea of starting a cryptography company. They pivoted to starting an encrypted payments company, with Elon Musk. They came into competition with a firm supported by Sequoia. After some antagonism, they were persuaded by Sequoia to merge 50:50, with the name PayPal. A couple of years later PayPal went public. Shortly after that Elon Musk was fired as Chairman. He walked away with $150 million.

In 2005, Thiel launched Founders Fund. This fund had a new philosophy. Instead of the VC bringing in an outside CEO, entrepreneurs would control their own companies. But Thiel went further. And I am quoting Sabastian Mallaby from his book the "Power Law". He cited the Pareto 80/20 rule. He observed that radically unequal outcomes were common in the natural and social world. It was therefore not just a curiosity that a single venture capital bet could dominate the entire portfolio. It was a natural law. He argued that venture capitalists should stop monitoring founders. The power law dictated that the companies would have to be exceptional outliers. Thiel felt that the founders of these outstanding startups were necessarily so gifted that a bit of VC coaching would barely change their performance. He found that the strongest performers were the companies that he had the least amount of engagement with. The art of venture capital was to find rough diamonds, not to spend time polishing them.

Thiel went further. He said that to the extent that VC coaching did make a difference, it might well be negative. When venture capitalists imposed their methods on founders, they were implicitly betting that tried-and-tested formulas trumped outside the box experiments. If the power law said that only a handful of truly original contrarian startups were destined to succeed, it made no sense to suppress idiosyncrasies. To the contrary, venture capitalists should embrace contrarian and singular founders, the wackier the better.

Entrepreneurs who weren't oddballs would create businesses that were simply too normal. They would come up with a sensible plan that would have occurred to others. Consequently, they would find themselves in a niche that was too crowded and competitive to allow for big profits. Because only handful of startups would grow exponentially, there was no point in getting excited about opportunities that seemed merely solid.

Mentoring had a cost, from the diversion of the VC's time from more profitable ventures, to the actual extra economic cost of this mentoring. Also, Peter Thiel has been quoted as saying "Get rid of non-performing CEO's and employees early. Leopards do not change their spots."

Founders Fund thus was a low-cost VC, that spent minimally on mentoring its proteges. They either sank or swim. On the other hand, Founders Fund had a record of funding a large number and a wide variety of investment proposals, the wilder the better, such as Uber. A significant proportion proved to be highly successful, making Peter Thiel very rich indeed.

As an aside, Thiel invested with Elon Musk on Tesla and SpaceX. To date these have been very profitable investments.

The next development in the Venture Capital industry was due to Paul Graham. While Peter Thiel was still rooted in the venture capital industry, although he spread his investments far and wide, Paul Graham made the jump into Angel Investing.

In 1995, Graham together with a fellow Harvard graduate student, started a software company called Viaweb, selling it in 1998 to Yahoo for $45 million of stock. He then turned his hand to writing, denigrating venture capitalists. "Spend as little as you can, because every dollar of investors money you will get it taken out of your ass". "What I discovered was that business was no great mystery. Build something that users love, and spend less than you make. How hard is that?". He was also strongly against large investments in startups. He said this caused dithering and distraction, and nervous VC's installed humourless MBAs to oversee quirky coders, much as the Bolsheviks foisted political commissars on Red Army units. Sweeping these criticisms together, Graham propounded what he called "a unified theory of VC suckage." "The VC is a classic villain: alternatively cowardly, greedy, sneaky, and overbearing." "When startups need less money, investors have less power….The VCs will have to be dragged kicking and screaming down this road, but like many things people have to be dragged. Kicking and screaming toward, it may be really good for them."

Graham, except for his polemics against venture capitalists, semi-retired. In March 2005 he gave a lecture to the Harvard computer society titled "How to Start a Startup". After giving his usual polemics, he was approached by two students, Alexis Ohanian and Steve

Huffman who had travelled from the University of Virginia to see him. They had a proposal to write a program that allowed people to order food by text message, and asked to have coffee with him. Which he did.

Four days later, Graham and his girlfriend, Jessica Livingston, were walking across Harvard Square, and he thought about his meeting with the two students. Why not help young founders by giving back? Set up an organisation to do a little bit of Angel Investing?

Over the next couple of days, the pair came up with a novel plan for seed investing. It would plug the gap that Graham saw in mainstream venture capital. At the time there was be minimal startup investment. It would be a summer school for aspiring entrepreneurs. They would all get together. Each participant would get $6000 to sustain them for three months of programming. They would also receive practical and emotional help; how to incorporate a company, open company bank accounts, and advise about patents. They would obtain feedback from the other participants, and there would be dinner once a week. The name of this organisation would be "Y-Combinator", which is a mathematical term for a circular method.

In the course of time, Y-Combinator grew and became a full-time organization for angel investing. It expanded to Palo Alto, and it is now located in virtually every major city in the world. Aside from concentrating on angel investing, another innovation was its total share of the startup's final share capital would be only 6 per cent. However, like the Founders Fund, intervention in the management of these startups would be strictly hands off. Aside from requested advice, it would be strictly sink or swim. Survival of the fittest. The struggling and unprofitable firms soon expired. The profitable went on to Series A, Series B and the IPO. Y-Combinator also profited from this process.

Between 2005 and 2022 Y-Combinator proved to be highly profitable, making a total profit of $14 billion. It was responsible, for instance, for setting up Airbnb. The success of Y-Combinator surprised Paul Graham, who is quoted as saying that this profit was "not intended". He had set up Y-Combinator for the benefit of intending entrepreneurs, not his own profit.

Since then, a number of copyists, such as Techstars, Seedcamp, Pioneer, and Entrepreneurs First, have set up. The latter company has sprouted offices in London, Berlin, Paris, Singapore, Hong Kong and Bangalore.

The question arises, why was Y-Combinator so successful? The answer goes back to Figure 24, The Power Curve of VC Profits. The essential feature of this curve is that while just a few of these new enterprises are wildly successful, there is a much greater number who lost money. Y-Combinator's success is due to the large number of potential entrepreneurs it attracts and fosters. Also, as described in the next Chapter, successful entrepreneurs create wealth. Entrepreneurialism is the source of wealth. VC entrepreneurs tap into this vast and perpetual source of wealth creation.

In Y-Combinator the initial enterprises get limited initial funding in the Thiel style, and unlike the original style of Sequoia Capital minimal resources are spent on management. If the original entrepreneurs prove incapable of managing their new enterprise from the start, and there is no rapid growth, most of the enterprises are allowed to fail. There is no patience nowadays for hot bath board meetings, pyjama clad get togethers, or eccentric founders; the curating of badly run startups has ceased.

To date, the Venture Capital industry has evolved a successful and viable methodology. From the original recruitment of a few isolated genius' at a restricted location, the Venture Capital industry has transformed into a form of mass production of VC enterprises. Profits are now just a matter of numbers. Many are called. Few succeed, but those few succeed wildly. The rest fall by the wayside – bad or incomplete ideas, bad management, bad luck.

Nevertheless, this form of investment has been found to be wildly successful for many VC entrepreneurs.

To summarise, the basic methodology of the venture capital firm is as follows:

Table 5   The basic methodology of the venture capital firm

1. The purpose of Venture Capital is to assist the entrepreneur to start a business to utilise his idea, and make money for both of them, by

providing startup capital, advice and maybe management.
2. The Venture Capitalist starts its business by setting up a VC organisation.
3. The Venture Capitalist advertises for/attracts entrepreneurs.
4. The VC sifts through applications. While early VCs were highly selective, the policy of Y-Combinator and the like is to be less selective, and to prefer original investment ideas.
5. Early VCs provided management guidance. The latest idea of Peter Thiel and Paul Graham is to provide minimal to no management guidance.
6. The aim is to get big fast, in an area where there is no competition. For that reason, the idea has to be original.
7. From the shape of the power curve, it can be seen that the major profits are made from the few highly profitable startups. The vast bulk of firms in the tail prove to be unprofitable.

Yes, ideas are cheap. Most are not original. But as Paul Graham says, among them are rough diamonds. The role of the venture capitalist is to expose this rough diamond, and to fashion it to create new wealth, not only for the venture capitalist and the entrepreneur, but for society as a whole.

CHAPTER TWENTY-TWO

HOW DO ENTREPRENEURS CREATE WEALTH?

This question is the basic question. Do entrepreneurs create wealth that did not previously exist? How is this done?

To explain how wealth is created, we need to go back to the question of the role of increasing returns to scale. In economics, everything goes in a full circle, and everything is interconnected.

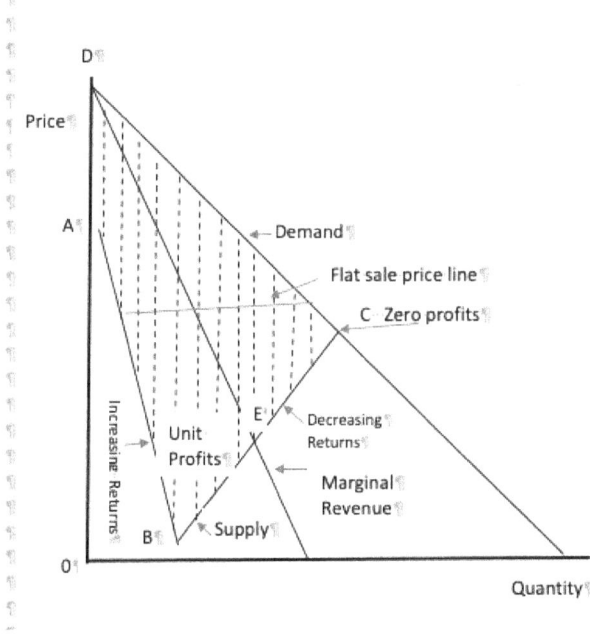

Figure twenty-seven — How Increasing Returns to Scale Creates Wealth

As the above diagram shows, the unit profit of a product is the length of the line from the Supply line or marginal cost line, ABC, to the Demand line, CD. From A to B, as the length of this line lengthens, the size of unit profits increase. Total profit at each point is the unit profit at that point times the quantity sold. This total profit does not reach a maximu until the Supply/marginal cost line crosses the marginal revenue line at E. Although unit profits are then declining the quantity sold is increasing. Unit and total profits decline to zero when the marginal cost line touches the Demand line at C.

However, as long as the firm stays on increasing returns, its unit profit increases – unless the Demand line is very steep, steeper than the marginal cost line.

126

A reader may be confused, and ask "Why have you advocated a flat demand line"? No, I have not, I have advocated selling at a flat price *below* the demand line. If you arbitrarily draw a flat line in the above diagram, above the marginal cost line, that line shows the unit profits until that line hits the demand line. You must not confuse the *flat sale price line* with the *market demand line.*

This raises the question, is aggregate wealth increased by entrepreneurial activity? Also, is wealth destroyed elsewhere in the economy when you make money?

In answer to the first question, If the activity of an individual entrepreneur creates wealth, then if there are numerous entrepreneurs active, then wealth is created by the sum total of all their activities. The more active entrepreneurs, the more wealth is created, if each entrepreneur creates a finite positive amount of wealth. Roughly, wealth is created in direct proportion of the number of active entrepreneurs.

However, the belief that there is a fixed quantity of profits that all the firms divide is total nonsense. Increased competition, while decreasing sales prices, increases sales. Thus generally total profits increase. Thus wealth increases.

In summary, one of the most certain methods of creating wealth is to start a new firm where the selling price of your product is greater than the price at which the product is produced. This is the most certain, the most universal method of wealth creation.

Yes, there are other ways to gain wealth. Speculation, thievery, conquest, and other non-productive activities such as litigation. Speculation has only 50% chance of success. It is a zero-sum game at the best. A well-run society reduces profits of thievery and other non-productive activities to a supportable maximum. (And that includes thievery by the government and the legal system!) As for conquest……In the past, when wealth was gold there was a chance. Nowadays, wars destroy the productive capacity of the conquered, and there is no profit in wars of conquest. Even wars to gain so-called "wealth" such as oil supplies have proved un-profitable.

The advantage from starting a firm that exhibits increasing returns to scale is that, as Paul Romer pointed out, growth is automatically built in. Only when the firm hits decreasing returns to scale that the firm soon ceases to expand. When the firm stops expanding, or hits zero profits, then management is forced to prune a bloated work force.

As Adam Smith wrote, 250 years ago, in the "Wealth of Nations", Division of Labour (increasing returns to scale), and sales to the extent of the market, is the source of all wealth.

So, to conclude, how do you become wealthy?

Become an entrepreneur.

That sounds trite, and you ask if there is a bit more to that?

Set up a business that operates under increasing returns to scale!

Being an entrepreneur contains a number of things.

1. You must be creative. You have to think of at least one original money-making idea.
2. You must be proactive. You must flesh this idea out into a practical scheme, and yes, put this plan on paper. If the idea is for a physical product, build a prototype.
3. You must be hardworking. Before the scheme gets going, and much more afterwards, you must put in a lot of hard work. Commitment.

Did I say, you must put in capital? The archetypical 'capitalist'. No, not any more.

There is a market for good original ideas AND, combined with, a person with character, who is willing to work hard and put the idea into effect. Even at this stage, the combined idea and a suitable person, is worth money, a lot of money, to Venture Capitalists. No, you don't need to put up any money yourself.

From that stage forward, as long as you continue to produce the product under increasing returns to scale, and sell the product at a fixed price, your firm will continue to expand rapidly. When will it stop expanding? For two reasons. You either hit decreasing returns to scale, which is really bad management, or you hit a declining demand curve ie falling prices.

If you hit the latter circumstances, your solution is to create a new or improved product, and then start selling it at a fixed price again.

A surprisingly high number of entrepreneurs get very rich, very fast. But even if you just become moderately well off; with hard work, good management and a modicum of good luck, you will become far wealthier than remaining an employee.

CHAPTER TWENTY-THREE

THE IDEA

Necessity is the mother of invention. But in a market, demand is the mother of invention!

Back in Chapter Nineteen, in the description of the Venture Capital process, Table 3 laid out a table of the Venture Capital process from the start to finish. Right at the beginning was "The Idea". The Idea is the inception of the Enterprise. This is the foundation of all growth, our standard of living higher than the level of starvation, and indeed all human development. Three hundred years ago most of humanity, including the West, lived just above starvation level. If you don't believe me, read Malthus (1820).

Ideas matter. Paul Romer said "What is the bigger obstacle to growth? A shortage of ideas or a shortage of things? It is a shortage of ideas."

The Idea, or more precisely ideas that are worth money, are the basis of civilisation. I cannot overemphasise this point. Human culture? As the saying goes, every poet has eaten once that day. It is the economy that matters most. And the function of the economy is ultimately based on ideas that are worth money.

I know earlier I said "Ideas are cheap". Yes, the production of ideas is cheap. It just takes a little effort, brain activity, and time. That is the only cost. But good ideas, once produced, are valuable. As Peter Thiel said, they have the value of rough diamonds. The value creation process starts at the point of the creation of ideas.

Some ideas come naturally. The spring into mind during a walk, as James Watt's idea did for the design of a steam engine. The unconscious mind is a major source of ideas. It has been found that if you think long and hard about a subject, the solution or idea pops into your head when you are sleeping, (like it did for August Kekulé with his Benzene rings), or during your awake moments in bed, (have paper and pencil beside your bed to record the idea), in the shower, or during walks. According to mythology, many ideas come in relaxed moments after a lot of thought.

But like all things, including the process of venture capital, an idea production process can be devised. Ideas can be produced on call. How does one do this? Isaac Newton described his method to create scientific ideas. He thought long and hard on a subject (often sitting on the side of the bed all night), and the idea pops into his mind. It really does work.

But if you have no wish to do this, a methodology has been described in a book, written by Andy Boynton, Bill Fischer and William Bole called *The Idea Hunter*, that applies method to the process of finding ideas. I shall describe it.

They hang their methodology on a skeleton or mnemonic, using the word IDEA.

I is for being Interested across a wide as possible area as possible, and draw connections. Be curious. Ideas don't spring to your attention on their own. You need to draw together many different related ideas. Put them together to solve a necessary problem, and you have an idea.

Albert Einstein said "I have no special talents. I am only curious". He brought together his interest in trains with the question of why the speed of light was the same in all directions, to discover Relativity.

On this question of interests, you yourself have a set of core interests, that Boynton et. al. call your "gig". This shortens your search for ideas. You gig is not necessarily your job, but what is your passion or purpose in life. What do I want to be? What do I stand for? What do I stand for? Does my work matter? Do I want to make a difference?

Is your vocation a source of joy? Is this something that taps into your talents and gifts? Is this a role a genuine service to the people around you?

D is for Diverse. This follows from the previous section. You need wide interests. Ideas are everywhere. They are like radio waves. You are surrounded by radio waves. You are surrounded by ideas. Tap into the universe of ideas.

One of the best sources of information comes from a diverse network of contacts – called 'strong ties' and 'weak ties'. Strong ties are family and close associates.

Weak ties are occasional contacts. Weak ties are more useful, as they have more diverse interests than strong ties. It has been found that weak ties are one of the best sources of entrepreneurial ideas. Chatting to someone at a bar can be more useful than talking to your family and close friends.

E is for Exercised. Work at it. You need to constantly exercise your mind, keep noticing things, thinking about what you have observed, and drawing conclusion. Do things. Don't turn off! Louis Pasteur said "Chance favours the prepared mind". Observe. Keep looking. Soon your mind will put two and two together and come up with an original idea.

Also, an additional tip. Write it down. Writing down your thoughts and observations and keeping them readily accessible is important. Ideas tend to arrive in bits and pieces and need to be put back together over time. Most people do not have photographic memories. It is an additional benefit that you go over these written notes, and try to put them together. Thomas Edison for example recorded thoughts in more than 2,500 notebooks. He didn't feel pressure to organise the notes immediately, but let his thought processes develop naturally over days, months, and years. He invented moving pictures by combining photos with thoughts on the spiral grooves of phonographic records.

Whatever is your form of note-taking, it is best to take notes when the observation is fresh in your mind.

Lastly, in this section on Exercised, *prototype* your idea as soon as possible. While a picture is worth a thousand words, a working model, a physical object (if such is possible), or a piece of working software, is worth many thousands of words. Imperfect though it may be, a prototype is a big step along the way.

All working inventions need to start with a prototype. Prototypes knock out unseen errors at an early stage. It does not need to look pretty. Just the idea is made to work. It also creates something that other persons can evaluate. A prototype makes the idea more understandable and allows people to offer feedback.

A is for Agile. A is the last letter in IDEA. Getting moving with the idea is more important than the idea itself. How many people get a good idea, but do nothing about it!

We come to the fundamental required characteristic of an entrepreneur, ACTION.

So, you get an idea, but it is too painful to take the next step?

Act!

What is your motivation? Answer the first four question yes, and the last no.

1. Do I enjoy spending time and energy on the idea? Lots of time and lots of energy. Go out there and talk to your friends about the idea (at least).
2. Deep down, do I really want to be a member of the project? (ie It is a good idea, but it is not

really my scene. I don't like getting my hands dirty, or giving people orders and making sure that they obey the orders).

3. Will I learn something in the effort? If you don't want to learn, go back to bed.
4. Do I want to be known as the person who brought the idea to life? Do you prefer anonymity? (Most do). Fame, even in a small area, may not be desirable. Some people may hate you, or may be just jealous.
5. Can I imagine a set of circumstances in which I would prefer not to be associated with this idea? Going back over the previous questions , is it a case of "I want the money, but not the job"?

Assuming that you answered 1 to 4 and 5 no, what do I do next?

1. Write the idea down. Describe it in detail.
2. Prototype it if you can. A physical working model/working piece of software is a major advance.
3. Obtain some Intellectual Property Rights, such as a Patent, Copyright, Trade Mark, what have you. In most countries the initial patent process can be quite cheap. Even software can be protected. At this stage see a Patent Attorney for advice. Not expensive, and well worth it.

Why go to all this trouble to obtain Intellectual Property Rights right at the beginning? Because there are denizens in the undergrowth who will steal your ideas. While the idea may not be worth much to you, to others the idea can be valuable, very valuable. Remember

Peter Thiel's rough diamonds. Once you have obtained Intellectual Property Right protection, you can be less paranoid. For most countries in the world, you are, to a degree, protected.

4. While you are doing all this, write a Business Plan. Business Plans are not described in this book. You can get this information in loads of other books. You just need a simple business plan. Keep the message simple. Focus on the possible benefits to the stakeholders.

As again, Peter Thiel says "...in these proposals I look first at the idea at the start, then I just glance at the business plan, and then turn to the applicant's C.V. at the end. The business plan is just to give an idea of the applicant's competence."

5. No, you don't need money, capital, management expertise etc. All these you can get from the Angel Investor/Venture Capital company.

Look around. Nowadays there are many different Angel Investors. (My favourite was Y Combinator, but as it has grown it has become more bureaucratic. Nowadays you have to do a three-month course in management at San Francisco, no less! You can do better).

If the idea is good and original, and well described, many Angel Investors can be interested. You will almost certainly get a generous deal.

From then on, your hand will be held. Maybe. Yes, you will have to work hard, but do what you are told. Act sanely and rationally. Remember the Venture Capitalist may be greedy, but he has your interests, as well his own, in sight.

After you have made your fortune, is this idea your last? Remember, while you are working for the firm, all the ideas you propose are owned by the firm. After you leave the firm, (hopefully after you have made your pile), your ideas are your own. The pot need not have run dry. Go through the process again.

CHAPTER TWENTY-FOUR

A STEP BY STEP GUIDE TO BECOMING AN ENTREPRENEUR

Firstly, after all that advice and information I'm not just going to cast you adrift. If you are going to sail off to the land of big bucks, you need specific advice on how to provision your boat, maybe some sailing lesson, and which direction to sail.

Table 6   What you need for a venture capital application

So what do you need?

1. The idea. It need not be a totally original idea, though it helps. But you need to be number two, at least, if not the first. The pioneer finds the routes and the water holes, suffers from the arrows, and stakes out the prime grazing areas. But you can learn from their experience, and stake out almost equally favourable ground.

    But, it is more beneficial to be number one. As long as you can learn fast. Rapidly implement necessary changes. And be capable of defending your market from late-comers - who are learning from you.

The idea is all important. Without the idea you do not even begin to become an entrepreneur.

You ask "Will the idea work? Everybody says that it won't work." Of course, they say that. Otherwise <u>they</u> will be doing it.

You are effectively saying "Will there be demand for my product or service?" Despite what the marketers say, there is absolutely no way to find out if there is demand for your product without setting up a firm and beginning to sell it. In economic terms "Supply becomes before demand". Or as the economist Jean Batiste Say said "Supply creates its own demand." I cannot guarantee that you will be successful at this initial step. As the first line in Table 1 says, 42% of venture capital firms fail because there is no demand for the good or service. That's tough. But you can't find out unless you try. (Also, your price could be too high. Remember, price above marginal cost and you will always make a profit).

So, right at the start, if you have an idea, you must set up a firm to produce it, and then try to sell it.

If you say "I have not got an idea." We..ll. There is advice in this book. There must be something in your experience where there is lack of supply. If you think about it, an idea is bound to come to you.

2. Courage. You need it. Becoming an entrepreneur will change your life, from the very start. That can be painful. It can be even more painful for your spouse, family, friends. You may need to change your environment, both physical and social. Your old life will be gone.

    Right at the start you will need the most courage. The risks will be highest. "My wife won't let me" I have found that is the biggest excuse. Bringing your spouse on board is a necessity.

    If your courage fails at this at this stage, there is a workaround. Nothing need stop you at this stage, after a bit of negotiation, proceeding with on-paper components of this project as if you intend to go ahead. Complete the paperwork and have it all ready to go. You can even apply to the Venture Capital company without committing to the final painful step. Tell your spouse that it is just a harmless hobby, and you could be doing worse things!

    In regard to your marital partner, it is a very good idea to involve them if you can at the very earliest stage. Two minds and hands are better than one. True, families come first. But nowadays women are told they need a "career". What better way than starting out as boss! As for men, I have found, unless they have a highly paid job, they need little inducement to get involved (and indeed, try to take over!).

3. Business Plan. This is a formal piece of paper the Venture Capitalist always wants. The Business Plan. There are two reasons for this. First, it shows that you have tried to think of everything, and everything is in its place. Second, the quality of the Business Plan displays your competence. If you are a total twit, and you can't do a Business Plan, nobody will give you any money.

    There are many books on writing Business Plans. Get one, and apply the information. I don't recommend getting someone else to do it. You will be questioned on the contents.

4. Your CV.   Most important. Most Venture Capitalists rate this as more important than the Business Plan. What are they looking for? First, any sign of dishonesty. Be absolutely straight and correct on the CV. Exact dates, reasons for leaving etc. <u>They will check</u>. Also, they will look closely for signs of laziness, ineptitude, insincerity... Remember they are investing in <u>you</u>.

Ok, after you have checked everything, ask yourself (and your spouse) do you want to go through with it? IF yes, send it off. There is nothing preventing you sending the application to several firms. At one time, (recently as ten years ago), there were few VC firms in the world and maybe none in your vicinity. But times have changed. If you live in or near a major city, there could now be half a dozen. Get a list from the internet and apply to all of them.

From the 80-20 rule, you probably won't hear from 80% of them. Of the rest, only one will be interested. Do your best to interest them. My strong advice is don't be choosy. What the Venture Capital firm wants it gets. Say yes, yes, yes, unless their requirements are grossly maleficent.

5. Lawyers. You need one. A specialist lawyer. Even if the venture capitalist is only making sounds that they are interested, obtain a lawyer at this stage. Yes, it is expensive. But not as expensive as not having one. You need also a lawyer that specialises in this area. How do you find one? Apart from Silicon Valley, there are few specialist venture capital lawyers around. But Patent lawyers have moved into this area. Obtain a list of the largest patent lawyers near you, and write, not telephone nor email, explaining clearly your need, and ask if they are interested. Write to several, and choose one that replies promptly.

6. The Venture Capital firms' procedures vary. But they will call you to see them face to face (at your own expense. That is why you apply to those located near you). If you are lucky, they will call you in again to sign things. One piece of paper most VC firms will ask you to sign is a declaration that this idea is entirely your own. If it is not, you should have told the VC firm that up front. Then they will want to see all your partners face to face. "What extent are you partners in this? Explain." All of you need to sign an agreement claiming a proportion of the idea,

and a disclaimer that there is no-one else. This is important. I have seen many legal claims from people that pop out of rabbit holes as soon as the business is valuable. How many of your partners will be "silent partners", and who will take an active part in running the firm? If there are too many of you, the VC will drop the idea, even if the others are willing to sell out. This situation is fraught for legal action. People get greedy later on. Get a good lawyer and get their agreement on paper.

7. You are offered a contract. Will you sign? Depart happy land for start-up land? The agreement has been written for you. Discuss with your lawyer (fast) to remove the wrinkles. But this agreement is often "Take it or leave it". Take it if you have any sense.

    The VC equity is nowadays on the average around 16%, but that can vary around the world according to the competition. For that they will give you money (in stages) and advice (my instructions – obey). But the money should cover your future salary. You can eat. The VC company will be experienced. "For this amount of money you will do this, this, and this. Your performance requirements are this, this and this".

8. Down to work. You need to start a company (to the VC specifications), hire staff and premises, purchase inputs, and get to work. Follow the VC

instructions, always, and the advice of this book, always.

9. Production. This requires a chapter of its own. Next chapter. This is the important part. If you produce nothing you cannot sell it.

10. Sales and pricing. There is a massive concentration in business of effort on marketing. Yet really good ideas do not need much selling. If the product needs large scale marketing, ie the product has to be "pushed", you are in a marginal business. Face it. In such a situation, either competition is too intense, there are too many substitutes, or there is not much demand for your product as it is relatively inferior. Back to the drawing board. You need a Gen 6 with a flat demand curve.

    More marketing, more sales reps, will not cure falling demand. Falling demand is due to a relatively inferior product. A sales rep is only good for one time only, getting new product on the shelves. If it doesn't fly, try something else. An advertising campaign is only good for a new product. Then intermittent, like the Wrigley gum company.

Finally, an excellent book for helping you setting up a business is: "How to Start Your Own Business....And Make it Work" by Cheryl Rickman, editor. DK publications. It covers nearly all you need, especially on the marketing side. However, its information about Production is non-existent. This is the same with the vast majority of small business manuals. They assume that the product you want to sell just pops into existent.

However, it is a very readable book. I shall briefly describe each of its sections. (The comments are my own).

- Making the big leap. If you are thinking about starting your own business, developing your idea in your spare time is a good way to start. Then weigh up the pros and cons, and understand your motivation for making the change. Its hard work and risky.
- Why you? Why now? When contemplating your own business, it is wise to do some self-assessment first. Take time to weigh your strengths and weakness, and consider if you are ready to be you to be your own boss. Being your own boss requires a wide range of abilities, many of which you will require at the outset.
- Coming up with your idea. Every business begins with an idea, whether to solve a problem or improve an existing product or service. A business idea does not need to be new, but it must satisfy a need in order to succeed. This book provides a useful checklist.
- Most businesses sell either products or services. Products must be manufactured. Services are provided by the actions of the firm. These are entirely different activities.
- You must find a need that is not currently met, *before you start the business*. You must assess the *appearance* of demand. Is your product *new*

so that it *disrupts* the market, and there is no current demand for it?

- Is your product likely to have a competitive advantage? Does it stand out? This has the advantage of both reducing marketing and reducing competition. (A good example is painting the soles of the shoes you sell red – yes, it happened very successfully in Paris.).
- Define your goals. If you don't know where you want to go, you will never get there, the cat said to Alice. Also define your values, such as honesty, value for money, passion, customer service.
- Choosing the business structure. Sole trade, partnership, company. Usually these decisions are not needed immediately, as many firms start as a sole trader and move though to become a company. Usually at a fast rate.
- There are many ways to sell. Early on, choose the best that suits you. From retail to the internet. In this get advice from professional marketers.
- Plan. Write the plan down on paper. Revise. Write it down again. If you want to really strategize, use the SWOT system. Strengths, Weaknesses, Opportunities or Threats. But remember, *any action, no matter how bad, is better than the best plan not put into effect.*
- Identify your potential customers. Only certain people will be interested in what you have to offer. These are the people to target. Do not be vague about it. Find out how much this *segment* is willing to *pay.*

- Assess demand together with Pricing. I have written a chapter about this. Briefly, you need a flat demand line. So, don't charge the maximum you can, but well under (as long as you cover costs), so that you can sell a *large number* at a fixed *price*. When the price starts falling, create a *new product* and sell on a *fixed price* again.

  As for pricing, I could write a further chapter on this. But many books have been written on the subject. (Books, books, books!). Your aim is to have a comfortable price, well above marginal cost, that can be sold with minimum marketing cost. A Cisco pricing system. Don't test the high prices. Even Gucci Bags don't have a high price (for them) but a standard price with which they can sell a large number of bags around the world. I can't give you more precise advice, as it depends on the product you wish to sell. Just remember the marginal cost, and the slope and position of the market demand line if you can find it.

- Where to base your business. Selecting the right kind of workspace for your business is an important decision. Start at the lowest cost place you can find, and remember, you can always move. Again, as I said in this book, moving production abroad is not always a good idea as you can miss out on the gains from *increasing returns to scale*.

- Is it a good idea to outsource? No. You lose control and gains from increasing returns to scale. The only reason to outsource is certain specialist activities are not large enough to provide scale activities, such as plumbing requirements. Do not outsource manufacturing of course, and also marketing. You may outsource IT and website design, sales and customer care, accounting, logistics, payroll, HR, recruitment. (These are called "cost centres").

- Financing your business. While a high proportion of start-ups are initially self-funded, I do not recommend going down this route. Raising money from a Venture Capitalist is far better. For three reasons. First, you get more money. Second, the money you get generally increases with your needs. And thirdly, and most importantly you receive expert advice, which you *must* take. No messing around. They are the experts.

  Sure, if you wish to contribute to the investment fund, or better still, start small, these both are very good options. But the Venture Capitalist not only has more funds available, but they are the experts at financing. They will know how much you will need, and when you need it. Their advice is worth more than any other the financing that you can obtain.

- Applying for Venture Capital investment has become standardised. You need three things. 1. A complete and detailed description of your Idea, in less than three pages. 2. A Business Plan, but not too long. This will be used for a measure of your abilities. 3. Your CV. Be totally truthful. They will thoroughly check, believe me. Be up front about any gaps. Don't extend employment periods or exaggerate your roles. And find the nearest Venture Capital firms (you will be asked to a face to face interview), and apply to several at the same time. One *may* respond.

Will they steal your idea? Unlikely. You must look at from their point of view. They are looking for someone to do the hard work. However, Patent what you can, and tell them.

- The Venture Capital firm and its manager are normally known as the VC. The VC will apply accounting procedures. But it helps greatly if you are familiar with Double Entry Bookkeeping. Both John D. Rockefeller and Warren Buffett said this knowledge was the basis of their fortunes. I recommend my book "Double Entry Bookkeeping" by Tim Walshaw. It is simple, basic, and comprehensive.

- Tax. Death and taxes are inevitable. Don't worry about it. If taxes are too much (along with other government regulations) move elsewhere.

- Staff. As you grow, you need to employ staff and employ a manager(s). This is a fraught area, and there are many experts, including your VC. When recruiting, don't be vague, and choose the first person with a nice smile. Write a job description, *and include growth requirements.*ie From the start, don't hire dummies, even if you have to pay more. Tip. If the firm is less than 40 individuals, you can manage it yourself. From that point, divide the firm, and hire at least two (carefully chosen) managers. From 150 persons onward, you will not know all the names. Carefully delineate managerial responsibilities. Divide the firm's operations. Specialise. Remember – increasing returns to scale!

- At this point, set up lines of communication, not only downward (the dreaded meeting), but upward. Upward communication, from inside and outside the firm, is absolutely vital. I have found the best means of upward communication is the Suggestion Box. Locked. Opened regularly and contents assessed by a special (highly paid) team called the "Secretariat". One person who uses suggestion boxes even supplies the Secretariat with neat grey pantsuits. They supply all the ideas they obtain from the boxes to the boss, for which the authors are well rewarded. But, there is a downside for these boxes. They are also called the 'tricotteur boxes'. They receive complaints. Often anonymous. "He groped me. He is stealing from the firm. He steals ideas, and thinks he can get away with it by sucking up to the bosses". After the Secretariat discusses the complaint with the boss, the offending party gets a visit from the girls from the dreaded Secretariat. There is also the system called "the Visitation", where a group of the Secretariat (as many as you can get) descend on a problem area. They start by interviewing the most junior staff first. By the time they reach the head of the area, that person is usually running around shouting and complaining and trying to get his friends to support him!

Unlike most other firms, this firm has had few internal problems. No angst, as far as it is known. There are a few teething problems when a branch is set up in a foreign country, and then everybody gets the message.

This firm also grows fast, always ahead of the curve, producing revolutionary new products on a regular basis.

- I could give you a lot of more detailed advice. But really this is the task of your VC. Most VC's will provide you with a manual, and all will have you supervised by a manager, who should keep a close check on you, and provide you with advice (orders) when needed.

- There are widely different opinions on whether you should be given management pre-training. Some VC's say that it is necessary and useful. Others have strong opinions that it is wasteful and a waste of time. I am in the latter category. But the jury is still out on this one.

Also use the excellent book previously mentioned "How to Start Your Business....And Make it Work". It provides a list of excellent advice.

- Any problems, see your VC manager. If that person is no help, go straight to the top. Most Venture Capital owners I know will welcome talking to you, when you can get past their obfuscating subordinates.

CHAPTER TWENTY-FIVE

ORGANISING PRODUCTION

The whole point of setting up a firm is to produce, and then sell what it produces.

The area of the production process is avoided by all self-help books, for the simple reason that the authors know nothing about the subject. Yet the subject of production is central to the existence of the firm. You <u>must</u> produce, manufacture, something to sell! That is an obvious requirement, and avoiding thinking about it will get you nowhere. So how do you produce a product?

I (even me!) cannot give specific advice on the production process of various goods and services. They will all, of course, vary. But one piece of employment advice. One of the very first persons you should hire should be a production engineer or an IT engineer, before you even start hiring an accountant or other paper pushers. Ask yourself, before hiring a person, is this person a "profit center or a cost center?" Get the production engineer's advice, and take it. Setting up a manufacturing or production centre is central to your firm's activity.

Table 7   Setting up production

Most of the initial money from your VC will go to set up your production facility.

1. Plan what you need to produce the good.
2. Buy or rent premises for production or manufacture in a suitable and convenient location. Good transport nearby. Comfortable and healthy. Office? You don't need an office. Never. Offices are a useless luxury. One multi-billionaire I know does not use a personal office. His desk is one among many others. He uses a meeting room for private meetings. Phone calls? They all listen in.
3. Start small. Employ few staff to initially build a prototype and test it.
4. Replicate the successful prototype and start producing it.
5. Sell it.
6. Marketing? If your product is any good, it will sell itself by word of mouth. Cisco Systems produced a software system that could make different software talk to each other. Demand exceeded supply. They had a production, not a sales, problem.

Production, production, production. Concentrate on production.

Remember Say's Law. "Demand will rise to meet Supply". From my experience it very often does. Supply, you will find, is the biggest problem.

Frequently, the VC has to pour money in for three years before the firm makes a profit. Setting up production facilities can prove very expensive.

<u>Warning on the need for increasing returns to scale.</u>

Suppose you decide that you won't manufacture this product yourself. Somebody else will. They will supply the finished product to you, and you will sell it. This is the error of many firms, large and small, from Apple to a large number of fashion brands.

In the case of Apple, for instance, it began to source from China. These Chinese companies entered into a fixed price contract with Apple, and sold products to Apple at a low fixed unit price, that Apple on-sold to the rest of the world. That in simple terms what it was, and is. Fixed price, fixed unit profit. Those who have read this book up to this point see the error of Apple's ways. **No increasing returns to scale**. Those genius business persons at Apple made a fundamental error. Yes, the firm made a growing profit. But this increased profit was **directly related to increased sales**. It did not increase at a **faster** rate than increasing sales. To put it another way, Apple was attached to a treadmill of innovation. Every year Apple had to bring out a new IPhone 5, 6, 7, 8, 9 and various varieties of each. As soon as sales for each generation began to fall, profits began to fall. There was no buffer of high profits.

What about Apple's Chinese supplier? It was reaping it in. It was operating under increasing returns to scale. With increasing sales, its profits were doubling, trebling, quadrupling. It kept very quiet about this. And yes,

155

Apple could negotiate lower prices from time to time. But the moral of the story is – by not manufacturing its products inhouse, no matter where, the US, Mexico, wherever, it handed most of its profits to outside the firm. It was fooled by the shibboleths of lower labor costs and an easy life.

Down at the level of yours truly, apparel and fashion goods manufacturers suffer from the same mistake. I know of many clothing designers who have gone for the easy life of transferring their production to China, and then more recently to Viet Nam and Bangladesh, in pursuit of the holy grail of lower labor costs. Do they set up their own factory at these locations? Never. They contract with a local firm. Fixed price. Sent back by the container load to be sold in the domestic market.

What usually happens? Everything goes swimmingly for a while. (I am thinking here of swimwear manufacturers. High quality. In demand around the world). They make big profits. The designer/owner buys a big house in a nice location. Then demand begins to fall. "Why are people failing to buy my high-quality swimsuits?" Because people are buying other high-quality swimsuits made at the same location, often made at the same factory, but sold at a lower price. A knock off. Sob! I'll sue!

Now, if the owner if this brand had set up a factory that they directly controlled to manufacture these swimsuits, (not necessarily in their home country), they

1. Would be operating under increasing returns to scale, and making higher profits, even though there may be slightly higher labor costs.
2. As the product is under their control they would be getting immediate feedback when the market changes (see the section on suggestion boxes) so they could change and improve in time. They save themselves from going bust.

What about setting up manufacturing in your home country? It is always preferable (at least initially) because:

1. The product you are manufacturing and the manufacturing process are both prototypes. Start small. Trial and error. These processes need to be under your direct control.
2. As you increase your output, carefully assess your process. Is it working?
3. Labour costs. Yes, there are countries where it is high. Where employing labour is difficult. But remember, you are looking at unit labour costs. These are often countries where productivity is high, and unit labour costs relatively low. Considering other managerial and marketing cost, the final unit labor costs may be relatively low.
4. Flexibility and feedback. You may need to change your operations suddenly due to changing conditions. Having your production located abroad makes it much more difficult to do this.

There are governments that do not encourage manufacturing in their countries. They say that they

want to reduce unemployment, but they are consistently anti-business, especially anti-manufacturing. High labour costs (together with government supported unions), high taxes, high electricity costs, high port and infrastructure costs…..
The list goes on. The manufacturer is just there to provide jobs for the workers, and provide tax.

I live in a country like that. It lives only by exporting resources, and taxing these exports, and has done for over a century. The profits from resource extraction are taken by the government and distributed to support high paying jobs and grandiose projects. As a result, the relative standard of living of the country has been slipping for over a century. But the people, the politicians, the legal establishment, one and all, continue to be content.

My advice is that you must always keep production under your own roof, whether it is at home or abroad. Always. Never contract production out, no matter how tempting it is. Otherwise, your contracted producer will end up taking all your profits, and eventually your market.

I know this is difficult. You will be going against the "best" advice. Cash flow. Lower labour problems. Supply problems. Etc. I sympathise. But if you succumb, you will lose direct control. If you send production abroad, someone will copy you. For certain. Yes, I know that they will do that even if you produce in your home country. But you will have a longer response time. Also, you can put a big label on your product "Made in……." That can double your sales.

Another piece of advice is, that if you are setting up production in a country, even your home country, with an excessive amount of government regulation or control, you need a "fixer" or "comprador" or the like. This person will save you a lot of expense and grief, for a relatively low price. No, I don't mean bribery, just influence. Even Denmark has an unnecessary number of regulations that can be worked around. In many countries there here is a whole industry called "lobbyists", who do more than lobbying. "Fixing" is a more apt word. It is well worth contacting those firms finding out what they can do for you, and how they can fix

a particular problem.

My strong advice is that before you start, you work backwards, and work out the production stage first. This should be part of your Business Plan. How are you going to make the product? Yes, in the process decide your intended market. This book will help you in that, and many other things. But remember, you cannot sell anything unless you produce it first.

CHAPTER TWENTY-SIX

CASH FLOW
OR
NOT SUDDENLY GOING BELLY UP

How many business owners are seduced by this refrain? "Inflation is higher than interest rates. I can't go wrong if I borrow. The government is paying me to borrow".

Especially among real estate developers. They borrow to the max on real estate that is increasing in value at the same rate or more than inflation. What happens next? They can't meet their payments. They have cash flow problems. They get foreclosed. Their bankers say "Thank you very much." Their business goes bust. Even though their the value of their assets exceeds their liabilities. Sell? Not in time. They need immediate cash.

Cash. Cash. Cash. Cash flow. That is the central requirement of any business. Not your assets. Not your contracts. Cash flow. If the flow of your cash outwards exceed you cash inwards, and you do not have a large enough buffer of Cash on Hand and Cash at Bank, you will go bust. Certainly. It is called Insolvency. Never mind the Balance Sheet, profits, increasing and promised business. It will vanish like the dew of yesteryear.

Talking of the balance sheet, the most important accounts are "Cash on Hand", "Cash at Bank" and whatever you call your current liabilities. The first two accounts are your insurance policies. Do they exceed expected cash inflows less expected cash outflows?

How can you measure that? You need a cash flow diagram. (Incidentally, accounting GAAP cash flow measures are worse than useless).

A cash flow table looks something like this:

Table 8

Expected cash flow. 000's

Month	June	July	Aug	Sep	Oct	Nov	Dec	Jan	Feb	Mar	April	
Cash flow in	110	125	130	130	135	140	145	150	155	155	160	
Cash flow out	94	100	110	140	130	130	135	155	147	160	150	
Balance	62	25	20	(10)	5	10	5	(5)	8	(5)	10	

In this exercise the accumulated cash balances exceed the deficits, in brackets ( ). Everything is fine. Keep it that way. You have control over expenditure. Your receipts are riskier and out of your control. Maintain a large cash buffer always.

The above cash flow diagram contains three things.

1. It is designed to show the maximum period you can fudge things when you run out of cash, before you go toes up, say a month.
2. From past experience, you need an assessment of the maximum amount of cash going out if you have no cash reserves. (This is desperate planning, but maybe you will need it). (Strictly

speaking when you are insolvent, and trading while insolvent is illegal…Sell assets. Desperately get loans if you are in this situation.)

You must have an accumulated cash reserve at all times exceeding the maximum expected amount in brackets (deficit) in the above diagram. Much more. Ignore advice that this amount does not get interest. Maybe there are a lot of goodies you can spend it on. Lock the cash away, and increase the balance from time to time. It is your scalp on line. How much should be retained? Well, Apple happily retains the equivalent of one year's revenue in cash. That policy has never done Apple any harm. In fact, they are now the largest banking company in the world.

Especially at the beginning of the firm's existence, cash outflows will exceed inflows. What can you do?

1. Plan ahead. Obvious. But the number of firms who do not do this are legion. Surprise, surprise, they are suddenly insolvent. So, estimate how much payments will exceed receipts, and when it will happen.
2. Turn to your VC. Ask for more money. Help! More planning is required. This is when, in the VC industry, the VC will either pull the plug, or will continue to support you. Phew! Begging and pleading will not help. Action! If there is a production delay, demonstrate that production will start at a definite day in the future. Hired too many people? You will have to fire a large proportion of them. Be tough. You don't need marketers, accountants, HR, executives…The VC

has seen it all before. They will make a list. Yes, a number of your favourites will have to go.

3. Short term fixes. Push payments to creditors out to a later date (with their permission if you can). Obtain short term loans.

4. Obtain fresh equity. The VC could probably go along with this. This is quite usual. Series A, Series B...

I hate to say this, but an un-planned cash flow problem is not only a reflection of, but is caused by bad management. You have been, as the management gurus say, sitting too much behind your desk with your legs apart. Drill down to what exactly is the cause of your cash flow deficit, and then <u>walk</u> down to the precise spot and talk to the people involved.

SUMMARY

This book is divided into Part I and Part II. Part I describes the theoretical aspects and Part II describes the more practical aspects of wealth creation.

I shall recapitulate what was said in the book. We started with basic microeconomics. The reason for this is that the budding entrepreneur must have a correct economics framework inside their head. Otherwise they will be seduced by the siren call of bad concepts, and will suffer.

Part I is a mini-economics course starting at the basics, but confined to a particular area, that part of economics that will be of most use to a business, that is the subject of Supply. It uses a lot of diagrams.

This section starts with the description of Supply, and how to describe constant, decreasing and increasing returns to scale of physical product, and so-called physical productivity. This description goes on to describe the more realistic curved line descriptions of returns to scale, and combines them into a logistic growth curve.

Then prices and costs are introduced to give a more realistic description of productivity gains.

The description moves on to the relationship between prices and Demand, and then the relationship between Demand and marginal revenue.

Marginal costs, or Supply in terms of prices and costs, is introduced, and it is shown that the firm maximises its profit when marginal cost equals marginal revenue. Also, where the supply line cuts the demand line, there is profit is zero.

We then move on to the essential part of the book – the definition of increasing, constant and decreasing returns to scale.

It is shown that a firm, to make maximum long-term profits, must operate under increasing returns to scale. When it operated under decreasing returns to scale its profits are limited.

How does a firm continue to operate under increasing returns to scale? The next chapter provides a formula, which if used, enables the firm to remain under increasing returns to scale. This formula also shows that no firm can operate under constant returns to scale as this area is too small to exist.

The next chapter shows that the optimum sales strategy for a firm is to sell at a constant price until it hits declining market prices. Then get a new product to sell at constant prices.

Part I finishes with a discussion of the relationship between revenue and a flat demand line.

Part II delves into the role of entrepreneurs, entrepreneurialism, Venture Capital, and the creation of wealth.

The first chapter of this section commences with a definition of Enterprise. That is Enterprise is the action to start a firm to produce and sell a good or service, and it is intended that this firm would operate under increasing returns to scale.

The book then goes on to discuss the definition of the Entrepreneur. "An Entrepreneur is a person who takes action to start a firm that will operate under increasing returns to scale to produce and sell goods and services". It is noted that an integral component of the above definition is increasing returns to scale. Without increasing returns to scale, an entrepreneur's firm would not create wealth for himself and society. The chapter then goes on to describe the essential characteristics of an entrepreneur.

This chapter is followed by the history of the name "Entrepreneur". It starts with Cantillon (1725), who invented the name. And then goes through Adam Smith (1776), and describes the demise in the use of the name and concept for a further 100 years until Alfred Marshall (1890), Frank Knight (1921), Schumpeter (1934) until Baumol (1968). From the 1980's there was a relative (relative to the past) explosion in the use of the name from Casson (1982) to Parker (2018). None the less, the comparison with total economics publications remain small.

We move on to Venture Capital investing. The venture capital firm receives proposals from persons interested in undertaking entrepreneurial activities from outside the firm, assesses them, and decides whether or not to invest in these proposals. If the venture capital firm does decide to invest, it goes through a standard procedure of deciding how to invest, and the form of this investment includes deciding on the structure of the investment and whether the venture capital firm would provide management supervision. This chapter describes the investment criteria used.

The next chapter describes the venture capital process, including the description of the framework of venture capital investing from Angel investing through Series A and B, to the IPO. This chapter finishes with a list of the usual reasons for failure of venture capital investment.

The following chapter is the history of venture capital from the start in Silicon Valley, California, in the 1950's to Paul Graham's Y-Combinator in the early 2000's. This chapter demonstrates the change in character of venture capital over the period, from the occasional investment in the 1950's/1960's where venture capital took as much as 80 per cent of the equity, to venture capital in the 2000's by Y-Combinator which takes 6 per cent of the equity. While the early venture enterprises often had management control of these startups, Y-Combinator generally does not bother.

The next chapter returns to an early question "Do entrepreneurs create wealth"? Yes. The reason they do is that entrepreneurs operate under increasing returns to scale. As such they operate under the average revenue (Demand) curve, and as long as they continue to operate under increasing returns to scale they continue to make profits, and create wealth. Since this entrepreneurial firm conducts generally a new activity, profits are not taken from other firms, but are newly created, out of nothing so as to speak. This new wealth not only benefits the entrepreneur, but society as a whole.

We then go onto to the core and the birth of an enterprise, the Idea. "In the beginning was the Idea…". This chapter states that all human development starts with the idea, and then goes on to describe a methodology to obtain valuable and productive ideas. The process is described in the book *The Idea Hunter* by Andy Boynton, Bill Fischer and William Bole. You start out considering an area that you are most interested and familiar with, your "gig". The book then goes on to use the mnemonic IDEA to hang the practical advice on how to create ideas.

We then discuss the concept of Production. It really should be at the start. If you don't produce anything you can't sell it. This is the forgotten concept in all advice books. Everything else, marketing, employing, management, all hang on production. So, not only work out what you want to produce and sell, but right at the beginning, *how* you are going to produce it, and in detail. No arm waving and wishful thinking.

From there we discuss Demand. The book discusses the Demand curve, and that it is the same as average revenue, and marginal revenue is derived from total revenue. From there we show that when marginal cost equals marginal revenue total profits are maximised, and when the firm operates under constant under constant returns to scale, profit per unit is maximised.

A particular demand line is accentuated, that all successful firms have to operate under. It is recommended that all firms should sell with a fixed price, when it hits the limit of the market, when the demand line and prices fall. It is recommended that this product is then replace by a new on, to be sold under a fixed price. The firm should always have a R&D department to create new products to be available tp replace the old product when it hits the limit to the market.

We finish with a warning about cash-flow. Insolvency, the lack of cash, is the final fate of all unsuccessful firms. You need to have positive cash flow always, or at least have a large cash buffer to cover your worst expected deficit.

The book ends with three Appendices. The first is s a proof that the marginal revenue is twice as steep as the average revenue line. The second Appendix is a proof derives the value of marginal revenue from the original formula for a change in revenue.

The final Appendix relates Enterprise to Paul Romer's model of increasing returns to scale, and through that the creation of wealth. Enterprise, Returns to Scale and the creation of wealth are ineluctably tied up. The value of wealth is drawn from the creation of wealth, and not from some physical stock value. This Appendix derives the concept of the Enterprise Quotient by adding the Enterprise Quotient E to Paul Romer's model, and deriving the relative values of Enterprise for selected countries.

CONCLUSION

THE ORIGIN OF ALL WEALTH IS ENTERPRISE - WHEN COMBINED WITH PRODUCING UNDER INCREASING RETURNS TO SCALE

A check list for getting rich is:
1. Create an idea for a profit-making product.
2. Plan how your firm will make this product, under increasing returns to scale. Write up a Business Plan, concentrating on production
3. Write an accurate CV.
4. Approach several local Venture Capitalists. Supply them with all the information they need.
5. Under the directions and funding of the chosen Venture Capitalist, set up the firm.
6. Under the directions of the Venture Capitalist, operate the firm.
7. Grow the firm until you achieve increasing returns to scale. Keep growing and dividing the firm into specialisations. Work hard. Look after the staff.

After that point you are rich!

Steps 1 to 6 are under the heading of Enterprise. Step 7 is operating under Increasing returns to Scale.

The origin of all wealth is *enterprise*. Enterprise is the activity of the entrepreneur, who starts firms and sets them running in the hope for a large financial return. These firms will be profitable from the start if the operate under *increasing returns to scale*, and remain profitable while they continue to operate under increasing returns to scale. The firms would cease growing soon after they hit decreasing returns to scale (caused by faults in internal management), or hit a declining demand curve; or as Adam Smith said, they hit the limits of the market.

After the subject of enterprise, this book is about production, and only secondarily about sales. You not only have to produce a good or service to sell, you must produce it with increasing returns to scale. Enterprise by itself won't make you rich. Producing under constant or decreasing returns to scale won't make you rich. Enterprise and production under increasing returns to scale are ultimately the *sole* source of new wealth and wealth maintenance.

You need to sell your product at a constant price until you hit declining prices. Once you reach the limit of the market, signalled by a declining demand curve with falling prices, you must introduce a new product, and start again selling that product with fixed prices. You must have a new product available always in the wings. That is why you have an R&D department. Not for public good, but for survival. R&D expenditure is an insurance policy. Those firms that belittle R&D quickly go under.

Information, from outside and inside the firm, is vital. I suggest using suggestion boxes and a Secretariat to open them.

Finally, the issue of cash flow. All expected cash flow, in and out, must be planned in advance. Failing to plan future expected cash flow is planning to go suddenly insolvent. Going insolvent is really, really stupid. Plan ahead with an expected cash flow table. Part of your plans should be the planned size of your cash reserve. You must have a planned amount of cash reserve always, even though it pays little or no interest, and you have a strong desire to spend it on something. The cash reserve is your insurance. Your firm will <u>not survive</u> without a planned minimum cash reserve.

Whether or not the reader is concerned with economic theory, the reader's eyes should be opened by this book describing how easy it is to get rich, how to create new wealth for themselves and through that, create new wealth for the community as a whole.

I wish the reader good fortune in his/her pursuit of entrepreneurial wealth, and I hope he/she benefits greatly from reading this book and by absorbing the message.

I leave with the cynical words of one serial entrepreneur. "Remember, if your firm goes bust, you will be the last to be fired!"

BIBLIOGRAPHY

Arthur, W Brian, (1994), Increasing Returns and Path Dependence in the Economy, The University of Michigan Press, Ann Arbor.

Baumol, William. (1968). Entrepreneurship in Economic Theory, *American Economic Review*, Vol 58, No 2, May, pp 64-71.

Beanhocher, E.D. (2006), The Origin of Wealth, Harvard University Press, Boston.

Blanchflower, D. G and A. Oswald. (1988), What Makes an Entrepreneur? *Journal of Labor Economics*, Vol 16, No1, January, pp 1-38.

Boynton, Andy, Bill Fischer, William Bole, (2011), The Idea Hunter, San Francisco, CA.

Brockhaus, Robert H. and P. Horwitz, (1986), The Psychology of the Entrepreneur, Ballinger, Cambridge, MA.

Buchanan, James M. and Yang J. Yoon, (1994), The Returns to Increasing Returns, The University of Michigan Press, Ann Arbor.

Cantillon, Richard. (1725), Essai sur la Nature de Commerce en General.

Carlsson,B. P. Branswehjebrun, M. McKelvey. C. Olofson, L. Perrsson, and H. Ylinenpaa, (2013), The Evolving Domain of Entrepreneurship Research, Small Business Economics, 41, pp 913-930.

Casson, Mark, (1982), The Entrepreneur: An Economic Theory, Barnes & Noble, Tottowa, New Jersey.

Govindaragan, Vijay, Baruch Lev, Baruch Lev, and Luminita Enach, 2019. The gap between large and small companies is growing. Why? *Harvard Business Review*, August.

Harbison, Frederick. (1956). Entrepreneurial Organisation, *Journal of Economics,* Vol 70, No 3, August.

Hayek, F.A. (1945), The Use of Knowledge in Society, *American Economic Review*, Vol 35, No 4, September.

Keyhol, T.J., D.K. Levine, P.M. Romer, On Characterising the Equilibrium of Economics with elasticities and taxes on the solutions to the optimality problem, *Economic Theory*, pp. 43-68.

Kiyoaski, Richard. (1992), Rich Dad, Poor Dad, Time Warner Books, Los Angeles, CA.

Klein, Lawrence R. (!977). Waiting for the Revival of Capital Formation. *The World Economy*, Wiley Blackwell, Vol1 (1) pp35-46. October.

Koch, Richard, (1997), The 80/20 Principle, Nicholas Breasley, London, UK.

Knight, Frank. (1934). Risk, Uncertainty and Profit, Houghton, Mifflin and Company, New York

Lucas, R.E. (1988), On the Mechanics of Economic Development, *Journal of Monetary Economics*, 22, pp 3-42.

Marshall, Alfred (1899), Principles of Economics.

Malthus, Thomas. (1820), Principles of Political Economy.

Marx, Karl. (1867), Das Kapital.

McClelland, David. (1961). The Achieving Society, Van Nostrand, New York.

Mill, John Stuart. (1848), Principles of Political Economy.

Nelson, Richard and Sidney Winter. (1982), An Evolutionary Theory of Economic Change, Harvard University Press.

Parker, S.J. (2018), The Economics of Entrepreneurship, Cambridge University Press, Cambridge, UK.

Ricardo, David. (1817), On the Principles of Political Economy and Taxes.

Rickman, Cheryl, editor (2021) How to Start Your Own Business....And Make it Work. DK Publications, London.

Romer, Paul. (1983), Dynamic Competitive Equilibria with Externalities, Increasing Returns and Unbounded Growth, Ph.D. Thesis, University of Chicago.

Romer, Paul. (1990a), Endogenous Technological Change, *Journal of Political Economy*, 98, pp S71 – S102.

Romer, Paul (1990b), Are Nonconvexities Important for Understanding Growth? *American Economic Review*, 80(2), pp 97-103.

Say, Jean Baptiste. (1803), A Treatise on Political Economy.

Sexton, D.L and P. Kassarda, eds. (1992). The State of the Art of Entrepreneurship, PWS Kent Publishing Co, Boston, MA.

Swann, Michael and William McEachern (2006), Microeconomics: A Contemporary Introduction", Thompson, Melbourne.

Smith, Adam. (1776). Wealth of Nations.sd

Solow, Robert. (1956), A Contribution to the Theory of Economic Growth, *Quarterly Journal of Economics*, 70, pp 65-94.

Varian, Hal R. (2010), Intermediate Microeconomics – A Modern Approach, Eighth Edition,   W. W. Norton & Company, New York.

Von Mises, Ludwig. (1949). Human Action: A Treatise on Economics, Yale University Press

Walshaw, T. (2013), Increasing Returns to Scale, Lulu Publications, Raleigh, NC.

Walshaw, T. (2017), Double Entry Bookkeeping, Lulu Publications, Raleigh, NC.

Walshaw, T. (2023), EQ The Enterprise Quotient, Lulu Publications, Raleigh, NC

Warsh, David (2006), Knowledge and the Wealth of Nations, W.W. Norton & Co., New York.

Young, Alleyn. (1928), Increasing Returns and Economic Growth, *Economic Journal*, Vol 38, No 150, pp 520-542.

APPENDIX ONE

PROOF THAT THE MARGINAL REVENUE LINE MEETS THE X AXIS AT HALF THE LENGTH OF THE AVERAGE REVENUE LINE

The definition of revenue is

$$R = pq$$

where R is revenue, p is price and q is quantity.

If we let the price change to p + Δp and the quantity change to q + Δq, we have a new revenue of

$$R' = (p + \Delta p)(q + \Delta q)$$
$$= pq + q\Delta p + p\Delta q + \Delta p \Delta q$$

Subtracting R from R' we have
$$\Delta R = q\Delta p + p\Delta q + \Delta p \Delta q$$

For small values of Δp and Δq, the last term can be safely neglected, leaving us with the expression for the change in revenue of the form

$$\Delta R = q\Delta p + p\Delta q$$

If we divide both sides of the expression by Δq, we get the expression for marginal revenue:

$$MR = \frac{\Delta R}{\Delta q.} = p + q\frac{\Delta p}{\Delta q}$$

Let's consider the special case of the linear (inverse) demand line.

$$P(q) = a - bq$$

The slope of the inverse demand line is a constant:

$$\frac{\Delta p}{\Delta q} = -b$$

Thus the formula for marginal revenue becomes

$$\frac{\Delta R}{\Delta q} = p(q) + \frac{\Delta p(q)}{\Delta q}\, q$$

$$= p(q) - bq$$
$$= a - b(q) - b(q)$$

$$= a - 2bq$$

Thus, the marginal revenue curve has twice the slope. As it has the same vertical intercept as the demand curve, its horizontal intercept would be half the distance from the origin, a/2b, as the demand curve, a/b.

APPENDIX TWO

WHAT IS MARGINAL REVENUE

For small changes in price and quantity, the change in revenue is given by

$$\Delta R = p\Delta q + q\Delta p$$

Where R is Revenue
      p is price
      q is quantity

If we divide both sides of this expression by Δq, we get the expression for marginal revenue

$$MR = \frac{\Delta R}{\Delta q} = p + \frac{q\Delta p}{\Delta q}$$

Or

$$\frac{\Delta R}{\Delta q.} = p\{1 + \frac{q\Delta p}{\Delta q}\}$$

APPENDIX THREE

ROMER'S MODEL OF ENDOGENOUS GROWTH THROUGH INCREASING RETURNS TO SCALE

Increasing returns to scale needed a trail-blazer, indeed an ice-breaker, that broke the pack ice of constant returns to scale, and led to the open waters of increasing returns to scale. Such a person was Paul Romer. If you look at Paul Romer's career, he moved from university to university. He never was in one place for more than a couple of years. Whether he was restless, or the moves were due to antagonism he felt from fellow academics, you will have to ask him. Yet starting in 1983, he continued to publish on the subject of increasing returns to scale. Romer (1983), Romer (1986), Romer (1987). It was not until Romer (1990), the paper called "Endogenous Technological Change", Journal of Political Economy, 98, S71-S102, was Romer generally recognised that he had produce something major. Jones (2019) stated that this was the "most important paper in the growth literature since Solow's Nobel recognise work." For this pathbreaking work Romer was accorded the Nobel Prize in 2018.

So, what was the novel insight in Romer's 1990 paper? It was not that he was just talking about increasing returns to scale. He had been doing that for years. But he nailed the concept of increasing returns to scale with continuous growth in the economy, by introducing the concept of the non-rival characteristic of ideas. Unlike physical resources, such as commodities and labour, that are rival goods, ideas are nonrival.

Rival goods are goods that have to be apportioned among the users. If one user has partial or total use of this good, then another user cannot use that part of the good that is already being used.

Nonrival goods are goods that can be simultaneously used by everyone. If one person is or has used this good, this does not reduce the use for everyone else. An example of a nonrival good is an idea. For example, if one person uses the Pythagorean Theorem, it does not reduce the ability of everyone else to use this Theorem.

An example given by Romer was the recently discovered cure for diarrhea, oral rehydration therapy. By just dissolving a few inexpensive minerals, salts and sugars in water in the right proportions produces a solution that rehydrates children and saves their lives. Once this idea was discovered it could be used to save the lives of countless children time and again.

But once you have increasing returns, output per person depends on the total stock of knowledge – a nonrival good. By implication, there are no physical limits to growth. There are no "Limits to Growth" due to constraints on resources, which was the panic in the 1980's. As Romer points out, in the United States, growth continues at 2 per cent per annum exponentially, and has for centuries, regardless. Long run growth is determined endogenously, which means that the economy produces more knowledge, which in turn produces more growth. Romer briefly discusses the possibility that people will one day run out of ideas, and that will reduce growth, but he cannot give a reason for that happening.

One theoretical result of Romer's increasing returns breakthrough is that increasing returns associated with nonrivalry means that a perfect equilibrium with no externalities does not exist. This result has a fundamental effect on the teaching of fundamental economics for students. Sooner or later, all those textbooks will have to be revised in a major way. See T.J. Kehoe, D.K. Levine, P.M. Romer (1992), "On characterising the equilibrium of economics with externalities and taxes as solutions to the optimisation problem", Economic Theory, pp. 43-68.

In other words, increasing returns to scale can also lead to the concept of multiple equilibria. Not the single equilibrium loved by promoters of pure competition. This result has major implications for macroeconomic policy. In an economy, multiple equilibria can exist, as the economy could, even would, be operating under increasing returns to scale, otherwise it would not be growing. Thus, if an economy is at one equilibrium it can be "jumped" to another equilibrium.

Keynes was instinctively correct on this point, but he could only describe his ideas in words. His opinions had no theoretical basis at the time.

Even though Romer in his Nobel Prize speech was very circumspect and did not mention multiple equilibria, in retrospect the multiple equilibria result will have a more far reaching influence than the somewhat theoretical endogenous growth theory. It will rapidly become a centrepiece of macroeconomic policy

But overall, Romer will be revered for his quiet persistence. He kept plugging away at his attempt to bring back the concept of increasing returns to scale to the centre stage of both economic theory and economic policy. For that, in the years to come, the world will be thankful.

Romer's model

The following is Romer's 1990 (Romer 1990) model, that is the basis of his further developments of the increasing returns to sale model.

We won't discuss the first two parts of Romer's paper, as they just form the introduction of his concept of knowledge as a non-rival good. In Part III he states that his model has four inputs, capital, labour, human capital, and an index of the level of technology. Furthermore, he separates the rival component of knowledge, H, from the non-rival component technological component, A. A can grow without bound.

The formal model has three sectors. The research sector uses human capital and the existing stock of knowledge to produce new knowledge. An intermediate goods sector uses the designs from the research sector together with foregone output to the producer durables that are available to produce the producer durables that are available for use in final goods production. The final-goods sector uses labor, human capital, and the set of producer durables that are available to produce final output. Output can be either consumed or saved as new capital.

Romer keeps the population and the supply of labor constant, the stock of human capital is fixed and that fraction supplied to the market is also fixed. Thus, the supply of the factors L (Labor), and H (knowledge) fixed. Final output Y is expressed as a function of Labor L, human capital devoted to final output H_y, and physical capital, indexed by an integer i.

I shall use a summary of all Romer's papers in Jones (2019) as it gives a clearer description of Romer's work.

As Jones says, the watershed contribution highlighted by the Nobel Prize Committee in Romer (1990a) makes three key contributions:

1. It identifies none-rivalry of ideas as crucial to econ0mic growth.
2. It highlights the role of profit-maximizing entrepreneurs and imperfect competition.
3. It places the key AK linearity in the production function.

The so-called AK model goes back a long way. A is an exogenous and constant productivity parameter and K is physical capital, but in Romer (1986) K was interpreted as knowledge, and in Lucas (1988) it was replaced by human capital.

In its simplest form, the AK model can be expressed as

$$Y_t = AK_t \qquad (1)$$

and

$$\dot{K}_t = sY_t - \partial K_t. \qquad (2)$$

Putting these equations together

$$\frac{\dot{Y}_t}{Y_t} = sA - \partial \qquad (3)$$

The growth of the economy is endogenously determined by the fundamental parameters of the economic environment.

As Jones said, the AK insight (i.e., a linear differential equation of the form $\dot{K}_t = sAK_t$ could generate an endogenous exponential growth rate) was the theoretical spark that lit a thousand lamps.

The insight that non-rivalry of ideas is crucial to economic growth led to a deep, intuitive understanding of the cause of economic growth. Instead of dividing the world into capital and labour, Romer made a more basic distinction between non-rival ideas and everything else (call them "objects"). Objects were traditional goods that appear in economics, including capital, labor, human capital, land etc. An idea is a design, a blueprint, a set of instructions used to generate more output.

Objects are *rival*; designs are *non-rival*.

From this, Romer demonstrated mathematically that nonrivalry of ideas means that production is characterised by increasing returns to scale.

Romer's basic production function (Romer 1990a) is:

$$Y = F(A, X). \tag{1}$$

Given a certain quantity of objects X and the set of knowledge A, the function F(·) gives the quantity of output.

Now consider the properties of F(·). If you multiply the number of objects of X by γ, where $\gamma > 1$, then

$$F(A, \gamma X) = \gamma Y \tag{2}$$

This is constant returns to scale. However, if you multiply the nonrival factor A by γ also:

$$F(\gamma A, \gamma X) > F(A, \gamma X) \tag{3}$$

That is, production is characterised by *increasing returns to scale*.

Each idea need be only invented once, and then it is technologically feasible for the idea to be used by any number of people or firms simultaneously and repeatedly.

Now how does increasing returns leads to sustained exponential growth?

With increasing returns, you no longer pay all inputs at their marginal product. This outcome, after over a hundred years of usage and assumptions, upsets economists. Romer (1990a) imported the concept of imperfect competition. The key to making these models applicable was the recognition that ideas, while nonrival, are no pure public goods.

Using this insight, the decentralised allocation in the Romer model features entrepreneurial researchers who hunt for new ideas because of the financial rewards that can be earned by innovating. Romer says that innovators are awarded a patent (I say the mere fact of increasing returns to scale) allows them to charge a mark-up over the marginal cost.

A third contribution of Romer (1990a) was to put the AK structure in the idea of the production function. Romer follows the notation that the stock of stock of knowledge is A, and reserving K for physical capital.

With A_t as the stock of ideas at date t, the flow of new ideas is denoted

$$\dot{A}_t = \theta H_{At} A_t \qquad (4)$$

where H_{At} is the amount of human capital devoted to research $\theta > 0$ is a parameter governing the productivity of research. There are increasing returns to H_A and A in this idea of the production function. New ideas lead to positive knowledge spill overs that raise the productivity of future researchers.

The economy is endowed with constant units of human capital that can be used to produce either consumption goods or ideas. Letting $s_t = H_{At}/\bar{H}$ be the fraction of the stock of human capital that is devoted to research, we can rewrite equation (4) as

$$\frac{\dot{A}_t}{A_t} = \theta s_t \bar{H} \qquad (5)$$

Profits incentivise people to search for new ideas. Equation (5) pins down the long-term growth rate of the economy.

In this way, the three key ingredients – the nonrivalry of ideas, the profit motive of imperfect competition (caused by increasing returns to scale), and putting the key linear differential equations in the production function – combine to generate the insight of Romer (1990a).

The non-rivalry of ideas makes sustained exponential growth possible. Romer was the first to truly understand the implications of non-rivalry – and the increasing returns it implies - for economic growth.

Adding the Enterprise Quotient to Romer's Model

The next section discusses of Paul Romer's (Romer 1990a) model, previously described. While this model is very effective in describing the relationship between knowledge, increasing returns to scale and growth, there was something missing. What was missing was motivated actions. Why was knowledge so readily converted into growth? Another question was that this model, like so many others, was U.S. centric. Why, if roughly the same amount of knowledge was readily available throughout the world, why was growth so different? The excuse that there were different levels of education in different countries was vague. Firms in these countries could still use the universal knowledge base regardless.

I propose inserting an additional variable into Romer's equations, the Enterprise Quotient, or E. This describes the amount of 'push' in each country to adapt new knowledge to business activity, and harness it to growth; or alternatively the 'spirit' of enterprise in each country. Those countries that have a low Enterprise Quotient would have a low rate of growth, while those that had a high level of Enterprise Quotient would have a high rate of growth.

Adapting Romer's (Romer 1990a) model

In Romer (1990a), Romer's basic production function was

$$Y = F(A, X) \qquad (1)$$

Now we change Romer's model slightly. Growth Y is also dependent on the product of the Entrepreneurial Push, or Enterprise, amount E, times A, the amount of knowledge.

This is because knowledge itself is inactive. It has to be used. Assuming that "exists and therefore it is used" is incorrect. There has to someone who is motivated to use the knowledge, and will actively use it. It is not enough to say that there is a profit incentive. There has to be someone who actively brings knowledge and the profit incentive together. There has to be an Entrepreneurial Push. I call this Enterprise.

So Romer's initial model is changed by including the Enterprise, E

$$Y = F(EA, X) \qquad (1a)$$

Then equation (2) is modified to

$$F(EA, \gamma X) = \gamma Y \qquad (2a)$$

Then equation (3) is modified to

$$F(E\gamma A, \gamma X) > F(EA, \gamma X)$$
$$(3a)$$

Again, the production that includes these activities of the Entrepreneur is operating under increasing returns to scale.

The flow of new ideas is now denoted by
$$\dot{A}_t = \theta H_{At} E A_t \qquad 4a)$$

Entrepreneurial influence increases the flow of new ideas.

We can rewrite (4a) as
$$\frac{\dot{A}_t}{A_t} = \theta s_t \bar{H} E$$
$$(5a)$$

The long - term growth of the economy is increased by the product of E, the level of Enterprise, in the economy.

I call E the Enterprise Quotient E.Q.

It can be seen that the explanation that growth rates vary between different regions is because of the different amounts of entrepreneurial influence between regions. Romer's model assumes that the quantity of knowledge A is equally available between different regions, and does not have an explanation to why it is not.

Quite simply the different influence of entrepreneurs between regions has been discussed by economic historians for generations. There are two major factors – the actual number of entrepreneurs differ, and the social and historical influences encouraging entrepreneurial action differ greatly between regions.

Applying the Enterprise Quotient E

As seen previously, Paul Romer's final equation (5) can be adjusted using E, the Enterprise Quotient, to be

$$\frac{\dot{A}_t}{A_t} = \theta s_t \overline{H} E$$

(5a)

Where	A_t	is the stock of ideas

$$\dot{A}_t \;=\; \frac{dA_t \text{ is the flow of ideas}}{d_t}$$

	A_t	= the amount of human capital devoted to research
	H_{At}	= the amount pf human capital devoted to research
	$\overline{H}$	= units of human capital that can be used to produce either consumer goods or ideas (constant)

$$S_t \;=\; \frac{H_{At}}{\overline{H}}$$

the fraction of the stock of human capital that is devoted to research

	E	= Enterprise Quotient
	Θ	= parameter $\Theta > 0$

Now when you include E, Θ is redundant.

So (5a) can be converted to (6).

$$\frac{\dot{A}_t}{A_t} = s_t \overline{H} E$$

(6a)

or

$$\frac{\dot{A}_t}{A_t} = H_{At} E$$

(7a)

as

$$S_{t.} = \frac{H_{At}}{\overline{H}}$$

Thus
$$E = \frac{\dot{A}_t}{A_t \, H_{At}}$$

(8a)

Thus, the value of the Enterprise Quotient is the flow of ideas divided by the product of the stock of ideas times the amount of human capital devoted to research. In other words, the enterprise quotient is directly dependent on the flow of ideas, and is reduced for a "rich" country having a large stock of ideas and a large amount of human capital devoted to research. However, this implies that the flow of ideas is independent of the stock of ideas and the amount of human capital. But it is likely that there is a strong feed-back from the denominator to the numerator. Not all that previous research may be useless. However, to the extent that the previous stock of subsidised stock of research is useless for the purpose of creating new ideas, then the Enterprise Quotient E is reduced.

Now, the question is, how can suitable proxies be found that equation (8) can be converted to a fraction that can be derived from existing data.

A proxy for $\dot{A}_t$ can be assumed to be the number of patent *applications* made in a particular country. This is different from the number of patents *approved* by each country's patent office. Firstly, the number of patent applications can be approximately the same as the degree of entrepreneurial spirit in the economy, while the number of patents approved depends on the rigorousness of the respective country's patent office. This can vary between countries.

Statistics show that the US Patent Office is the most rigorous, rejecting the highest proportion of patent applications, while other countries such as Australia reject a smaller proportion of patent applications. Thus, the number of patents accepted is likely to be a poor proxy of the amount of enterprise in the country.

In regard to the ratio $\dot{A}_t / A_t$, unfortunately no patent office around the world seems to publish figures for the current stock of active patents A_t. There is no figure for the relationship between the number of patent applications and the stock of active patents.

The best proxy for this ratio appears to be the proportion of patent applications to number of the country's population. The higher this proportion, the higher the likely value of $\dot{A}_t / A_t$. Let's call this proportion

$$B = \frac{\dot{A}_t}{population.} \qquad (9a)$$

B has to be related to the quantity H_{At}, the amount spent on research, or R&D expenditure. As the size of a country increases, generally more is spent on research. This has to be brought into a simple relationship, so different countries can be easily compared. The simplest way to do this is to divide H_{At} by the GDP of each country. Lets call this variable

$$C = \frac{H_{At}}{GDP.} \qquad (10a)$$

$$E = \frac{\dot{A}_t}{A_t \, H_{At}} \qquad (11a)$$

Modify (8a) to derive the common ratio of E for each country.

$$E = \frac{B}{C} \qquad (12a)$$

From statistical data, E can be calculated for different values for a number of different countries in the following table:

Table 9 → Calculating the Enterprise Quotient for various countries

COUNTRY	R&D EXPENDITURE AS A % OF GDP	NUMBER OF PATENT APPLICATIONS	POPULATION	PATENT APPLICATIONS /POPULATION	E ENTERPRISE QUOTIENT	E x 10³
	C			B	B/C	
USA	3.38	595,780	339,123,510	0.01757682	0.0051976	5.20
CHINA	2.44	1,585,667	1,425,840,886	0.001112098	0.00045578	0.46
UK	2.4	58,410	67,736,806	0.00086230	0.0003592	0.36
CANADA	1.7	77,165	38,781,806	0.0009583	0.000563	0.56
AUSTRALIA	1.83	33,409	25,978,935	0.0014399	0.0007868	0.79
FRANCE	2.35	72,800	64,256,584	0.0011329	0.000482	0.48
GERMANY	3.1	173,220	83,294,637	0.0020796	0.000670	0.67
INDIA	0.7	61,573	1,432,338,288	0.0042987	0.0061410	6.1
MEXICO	0.3	1305	128,455,567	0.0001315	0.000338	0.33
JAPAN	3.26	727,348	123,454,567	0.0589167	0.0180724	18.07

The implication of this table is that if a country does not make a full use of its R&D, its enterprise quotient would be low. A high rate of R&D does not guarantee a high enterprise quotient. On the other hand, a country like

India that has a limited amount of R&D but has a high proportion of patent applications has a high Enterprise Quotient E.

E is the proxy for the entrepreneurial spirit of each country. Of course, it does not cover total entrepreneurial activity in areas not covered by R&D, such as starting up shops, trucking companies and so on. Maybe suitable proxies for these activities can be found from further research.

Nevertheless, these results are interesting. It is not surprising that Japan is shown to be the most enterprising economy, with an E of 18.07. What is surprising is that India has an E that comes second, with an E of 6.1. The USA has an E of 5.20, despite its vast expenditure on R&D. China is shown to have an E of 0.46, an average level of enterprise activity, despite its high level of R&D activity. The UK shows a relatively poor level of entrepreneurial activity with an E of 0.36, around the same level as Mexico with an E of 0.33.

As has been said, the measure of E does not reflect areas of enterprise not related to R&D, such as starting shops and similar small-scale enterprises. More research needs to be done to find proxies for these activities.

www.ingramcontent.com/pod-product-compliance
Lightning Source LLC
Chambersburg PA
CBHW071547200326

41519CB00021BB/6645